A MIXED HARVEST
STORIES OF NEW MILLS

A MIXED HARVEST
STORIES OF NEW MILLS

by Maurice Hope

Foreword by Sir Martin Doughty

breedon **books**
PUBLISHING

First published in Great Britain in 2003 by
The Breedon Books Publishing Company Limited
Breedon House, 3 The Parker Centre,
Derby, DE21 4SZ.

ISBN 1 85983 369 1

Printed and bound by Butler & Tanner,
Frome, Somerset, England.

Cover printing by Lawrence-Allen Colour Printers,
Weston-super-Mare, Somerset, England.

Contents

Dedication

To Pete

Sketches by Cath Hope.

Acknowledgements

AS may be seen from my references, I am indebted to the New Mills Local History Society, without whose publications *A Mixed Harvest* would not have been possible, and I am more than happy to acknowledge the writings of O.D. Bowyer, D. Brumhead, R. Bryant, J. Humphreys, J. Powell, J.V. Symonds and R. Weston in this regard. I also thank the Society for the use of photographs from their archive.

In my wartime chapters, Stephen Lewis's *Debt of Honour* was an indispensable source of biographical information, while Sir Martin Doughty's *The Town Under the Park* proved invaluable in my references to the Torrs Riverside project. I am grateful to them both.

From time to time I have also relied heavily upon *The High Peak Reporter*, and upon *New Mills 1894–1994* and other Council publications.

On a more personal level – 'in the field', so to speak – my search has been long and fascinating, and has taken me into the homes and workplaces of scores of local people who have provided written materials, photographs, documents and anecdotes. Their generosity and support have been extraordinary, and I would particularly like to thank Peter Bailey, Bill and Jean Barton, Peter Beardswood, Elaine Bowden, Roger Bryant, Jane Butterworth, George Cooper, Beverley Critchlow, Carolyn Dent, Graham Dent, Reg Dorsett, Sir Martin Doughty, Geoff Griffiths, Maurice Hallam, John Hemsworth, Sue Heywood, Christine Howe, Evelyn Hulse, John Humphreys, Allan Jones, Derek Jones, Philip Kendall, Stephen Lewis, Lorrie Marchington, Anne and Ian Mason, Adrian Matlow, Trevor Matlow, Karen Morris, Angela Peatfield, Bill Robertson, Lesley Stafford, Susan Stevens, Jim Thompson, George Waterhouse, Alan Wilks, David Williamson, Gary Wood and Lynne Woodward.

I am most grateful to local historians Barbara Matthews and Derek Brumhead who read my draft text and made many constructive suggestions; to my daughter Cath for her delightful sketches; to Lynda Purnell who has somehow managed to transform my scribble into neat copy; and to the ever-cheerful and obliging staff of New Mills Library, Gwenda Culkin, Kath Dent and – once again – Barbara Matthews, whose enthusiasm for the project has been boundless.

Finally, I am deeply indebted to Margaret my wife, both for her shrewd professional eye and, most of all, her unwavering encouragement.

Maurice Hope

Foreword

Sir Martin Doughty

THE history of New Mills is better chronicled than in most small towns thanks to the enthusiasm of the Local History Society and the interest generated by the Heritage and Information Centre and the Library.

Yet history derived from the likes of published accounts, burial records or official registers can often be dry and academic.

Maurice Hope's excellent book is different. It puts facts, events and buildings into storylines with real local people as the storytellers. It is above all about people who, over the generations, have lived and breathed New Mills and made their own personal contribution to life in a small High Peak market town.

This is no sanitised treatise. In fact it would be difficult to write one about New Mills without taking out some of the best stories. The book is all the better for including the unsavoury alongside the savoury, the things some would wish to forget along with the memorable.

When I was growing up in New Mills in the

The Millennium Walkway, above Torr Vale Weir. (Photo © Gary C. Wood, 2003)

...Clinging to the wall.
(Photo © Gary C. Wood, 2003)

1960s it was genuinely a mill town, with the humour of the shop floor making the daily grind bearable for many. Now, with the bleaching and dyeing industry gone, out-commuters, often public sector, rub shoulders with local manual workers. The mix can be eclectic. Look at the shops. The Alternative Health Clinic next to the bookies, Bronze Bodies by the bookshop, the tattooist next door to the Victorian fireplace shop. Sort of Royston Vasey meets UMIST professor.

Some shops though, have been more enduring. Maurice Hope looks back with affection on the more than 200 years combined service to the town of a quartet of shopkeepers. But would anyone wager that the next generation will see the same, with the sort of pressures now facing traditional market town centres?

Of course, Maurice does not ignore the buildings and structures, for they have every chance of being the most enduring. New Mills will survive as a community if it has a sense of place. And it is the bridges – what Roy Hattersley calls our Victorian spaghetti junction – and the Torrs gorge and river valleys which they span, which are unique.

Not everyone has a park under the town, still less a millennium walkway.

THE TORRS MILLENNIUM WALKWAY, NEW MILLS, DERBYSHIRE

In celebration of the millennium walkway.

Introduction

market street.

QUITE frankly, driving through New Mills can be more than a little annoying.

Coming in over the tops along the old packhorse route from Mellor, the approach to the White Hart Inn – often half-choked with alternate ranks of stationary cars – can stretch even the mildest of dispositions to breaking point.

Add to this the comings and goings of the erratic shoppers of Market Street, the mischievous antics of the delivery-making, double-yellow-line squatting, U-turning fraternity, not to mention the impassive yet ruthless speed ramps, the awkward mini-roundabout at Foy's corner, and the ceaselessly blinking pelican crossing – given all these impediments, one can easily understand the average motorist's tendency to regard a journey through New Mills as one of life's troublesome

Coming into New Mills over the tops from Mellor.

Bridges, seeming to grow from the landscape itself.

little challenges, and the junction at the foot of Union Road as a happy release, a welcome gateway to a better world!

In such a context – locked in traffic perhaps, stuttering ahead, stopping, moving on again – one might easily empathise with a motorist's view of New Mills not only as an uncooperative sort of place but also – and how can we put this kindly? – a rather dreary one. Grey and routine. Higgledy-piggeldy, with cluttered streets, a modest and uneventful little centre, and nothing much to boast about. Take Union Road for example: a line of tidy but lacklustre shops and offices, a couple of decent public buildings, a police station, a pub and a set of traffic lights. The very embodiment of the prosaic!

Yet occasionally, to pass away one's traffic-locked time, it can be good to speculate. Things are not always what they seem... There can be more to places than meets the eye... The

unassuming aspect of Union Road might be an illusion! A mere façade obscuring an extraordinary hinterland! It might not be that New Mills has nothing to boast about, but simply that she does not care to boast...

–oOo–

We are strolling through a narrow, densely wooded gorge. To our left is a fast-flowing river, to our right are tall, sandstone cliffs, chipped and sculpted, sometimes into steep, smooth faces, sometimes into dark ledges strewn with trees and wild tangled bushes. Farther along the path a second river meets with the first. Augmented, the river rushes on, over weirs, plunging into seething pools, and snaking around the elbow of the gorge. Its noise is amplified by the sheer cliffs. Nearby, steep paths lead up to the top of the high rocks.

Down on the valley floor there are old walls

and iron grilles, stone steps and arches, while all around, bridges – massive or compact, reaching high or lying low – straddle the gorge, or broach its streams. Made from the sandstone of the Torrs the bridges seem to grow from the landscape itself. One – some distance from the others – breaks away and strides across the floodplain beyond the gorge in 13 giant steps.

Downstream, the river passes, on the far side, an old mill, its roofline and tall chimney sprouting green ferns and grasses, its face half hidden by a screen of ivy. Its many windows gaze across to a huge man-made wall, which rises almost vertically from the water.

And here – sometimes clinging to the wall and sometimes standing free – a long, elegant stainless steel walkway, high above the river, sweeps dramatically around the curve. It disappears into the woods beyond the mill, and all around trees climb towards the cliff tops.

The contrasts here – in colour, texture, materials; between natural and man-made, old and new – are quite extraordinary. Theatrical almost. And the landscape, though not of myth and legend, would need only a small step in one's imagination to become so. Maybe river sprites would then rise from the raging waters, and dragons spit fire from the mysterious shadows.

And should we ascend from these half-lit depths to the rim of the gorge, what might we find standing above us? A mediaeval castle? A glittering palace? The ancient walls of a forgotten city? No. None of these. Above we would find Union Road.

Torr Vale Mill, gazing across the River Goyt.

Chapter 1
Theatre of Change

Torr Mill.

and rectangular window leading the eye to a stone bridge lying low, and a taller bridge behind. It is such an agreeable picture, made even more so by the curving weir in the foreground, and the Goyt's rocky outcrops beyond. In the summer, when the foliage is dense and the light is mellow, the scene is for all the world like one of those sentimental, not to say voluptuous, etchings so treasured by our Georgian and Victorian ancestors.

But wait! Should those ancestors have stood on this very spot, they would have experienced a quite different vision. For in those days this was no earthly paradise, it was an engine room of the Industrial Revolution.

–oOo–

THE Torrs Riverside Park, whose gorge half-encircles Torr Top, is now a magnet for visitors from near and far.

It is a fascinating place, filled with an almost tangible sense of the past. Yet, because it is tranquil and beautiful and spectacular all at once, it is perhaps too easy for the visitor to gain a fanciful and distorted view of what it was like in earlier times.

Let us stand for a few moments beyond the Millward Memorial Bridge, for example, and look back across the confluence of the Sett and the Goyt towards what remains of Torr Mill – its outer wall seemingly castellated, its rounded arch

Towards the end of the 18th century entrepreneurs and engineers had eagerly surveyed these lively streams and the rock shelves behind them. Although, as the ancient paths and low bridges would have suggested, access to the gorge would be difficult, and movement restricted, the wide, firm terraces a few feet above the rivers would enable substantial building to be undertaken. So, even though this may not have represented an ideal site, its potential for industrial development could neither be denied nor resisted. Particularly in the exciting new age of textile manufacture.

The prospectors returned again and again.

The Torrs Riverside Park near the confluence of the Sett and Goyt. (Photo © Gary C. Wood, 2003)

They measured, calculated, speculated and then began to hack and chisel the cliffs, uproot the trees and redraw the rivers. In a cauldron of ambition the gorge was attacked from every angle until it became a harsh and impatient place, stripped of beauty and filled with purpose.

Yet although the gorge may have been virgin territory for the developers, industrial enterprises were already established nearby. Beside the river Sett, a short distance upstream from its meeting with the Goyt, Barnes Paper Mill – or Barnes Top Shop as it later became – had been plying its trade since the 1730s. While farther upstream again, Beard (woollen) Mill – or Hyde Bank – had been at work since the 16th or 17th century. As for the very first cotton mill in the region, this had taken its place beside Beard Mill in 1785 and the two mills had operated together until the closure of the woollen mill in about 1799.

Compared to a site near Salem Mill, however, these were merely fledgling industries. For at Salem, where the gorge widens out and an ancient bridge crosses the Sett, a manorial mill – administered by the Duchy of Lancaster – had established a right to grind corn for local inhabitants as far back as the late 14th century! Indeed, sometime after 1391 the corn mill became known as 'Newmylne', thereby providing the name for the modern town.

It was against this background that in the late

The picturesque ruins of Torr Mill. (Photo © Gary C. Wood, 2003)

18th century, three water-powered cotton mills – Torr Vale Mill, Rock and Torr Mills – were built in the narrowest and deepest part of the gorge. Of these three, Rock Mill and Torr Mill now lie in ruins, while Torr Vale Mill, having been continuously occupied since its opening in 1788, ceased production only at the turn of the millennium.

Rock Mill is situated at the foot of one of those steep and now picturesque paths that leads up to the town, while Torr Mill occupies a more congenial site on the level ground near the junction of the rivers.

And what tales these mills would tell if only they could! Torr Mill, tales perhaps about the Schofields who commissioned its construction, about peaceful beginnings, and a devastating awakening by fire in 1838. It would enthuse about its conversion from water to steam power, and of the building of its great chimney in 1846 – a chimney which, projecting above the lip of the gorge, would spew clouds of black smoke over Torr Top. We would hear about works teas at the Queens Arms Hotel, the tragic drowning, in 1860, of a young girl, and about angry injunctions against the Union Road bridge builders who had

The 'bottom' of New Mills – an ancient crossing of the River Sett. (Photo © Gary C. Wood, 2003)

carelessly blocked the river. There would be cottage and town and church gossip, tales of hardship and poverty, of Co-operative funding withdrawals, and of disastrous financial dealings. And finally – and here the mill would show us the charred timbers to substantiate its tale – we would hear about the terrible fire of 1912 that reduced it to a shell, and how it lay there untended for 60 years.

Rock Mill too would claim a fair share of ups and downs: a hopelessly optimistic 999-year lease; a dynasty of remarkable Crowthers (and indeed Crowders), Edges, Yates, Oldhams; beautiful daughters and solemn sons; a river deeply polluted by the printers of Furness Vale and Whaley Bridge, and the blaze of 1846 sparking and swirling in the Torrs wind; a marvellous six-colour calico printing machine and conversion to paper manufacture; equivocation, bankruptcy, abandonment, and a mill estate lying in neglect until 1974.

Torr Mill. (Courtesy John Hemsworth)

The sturdy remains of the Torr Mill chimney.

over with bales and timber, pushing through the crowds.

–oOo–

There is at once an archaic and yet timeless quality about the Torrs that in a sense epitomises the town above. Is it old, is it new? Who can tell? Yet consider the foundation dates set into the façades – Jubilee Buildings 1887, the Masonic Hall 1894 – and one realises that the area is in fact a 'modern' creation. Indeed, with the exception of a handful of buildings – such as the so-called weavers' cottages in Rock Street – most of it has come about in less than two human life spans. Step back one more life span, and one can accommodate most of the remainder of New Mills. Perhaps it is the weathered stone or even the play of light that belies the truth. Or perhaps it is the weight of a history which has seen New Mills diced, quarried, tunnelled under, reshaped and sometimes recklessly exploited, that gives the town its well-matured appearance.

–oOo–

And the history of Torr Vale Mill would be no less eventful, although it is quite likely that – notwithstanding the weavers' shed fire of 2001 – she would prefer to concentrate not upon stories of yesterday, but of today. For not only has Torr Vale Mill managed to battle through more than two centuries of industrial endeavour – her bobbins, throstles, mules, dhooties and sateens providing in the process a veritable lexicon of textile manufacture – but she has even contrived to reach the 21st century with a glimmer of hope for some kind of future development.

These then, were the mills of the Torrs, centres of manufacture, debate and conflict; surrounded by noise and smoke and smell; by workers young and old cramming the pathways, steaming chain horses clip-clopping on slippery cobbles and clattering carts spilling

As for the more distant past, it is often reported that the area now known as New Mills was once contained within the Royal Forest of the Peak, and that in the 13th century certain parts of that forest were acquired for farming activities. Milling operations were established in the late 14th century and, in due course, for reasons of taxation, four of the 10 scattered hamlets that comprised Bowden Middlecale (the local administrative centre), joined together. One day these four – Beard, Ollersett, Thornsett and Whitle – would become New Mills, but that would not be until 1876 – a long way ahead.

In the meantime cattle and sheep farming

Torr Vale Mill from Rock Mill Lane. (Photo © Gary C. Wood, 2003)

became more widespread, weaving and spinning were practised in some of the farms and cottages and coal pits were opened up on the wind-tossed moors.

This, then, became the place where Thomas Beard would make his cloth and where Edward Bowden would tailor splendid suits for Sunday best; where William Dewsnap of Bald Beard

would cobble his shoes and Anthony Gregory of Thornsett Hall bake bread for his customers' table.

Rightly or wrongly, a sense almost of acquiescence emerges from these times; of a region where the essentials of life are still dictated by the seasons. Not that it would have been easy or peaceful. There would always have been disagreements and feuds – with authority, employers, neighbours, within and between families – always jealousy and inequity, contests for land, money, power. Yet even so, it may have been a place where people had at least some measure of control over circumstances, and perhaps over the tempo and character of change.

Along the River Sett, looking towards the weavers' cottages on Rock Street. (Photo: Andy Lawson)

Above the Torrs – timeless New Mills.

Burn'd Edge Number 2 Pit, or new Pingot, in the late 19th century. (Courtesy John Hemsworth)

One day, however, in this very spot – though not just yet – the thrust of industrial enterprise would impose its own rules and maxims. It would think nothing of plundering the lives of those who had fought hard for the right to farm the land, and of claiming for itself all of the resources it could lay its hands on.

Yet even at the very end of the 18th century it would have been impossible to have known this. How could the farmers and tradesmen and cottage weavers of that time have foreseen that the planners and engineers whom they watched dividing the valley of the Torrs and rechannelling its streams, were no less than agents for a new protocol, ambassadors of irresistible forces that would change the route of history itself? How could they have guessed that one day a network of roads, railways and canals would surge across the fields, and that factories and machines, built by agents such as these, would change the face of the whole nation – indeed, of the world?

And how could they have known that they themselves would be an essential element in the equation, and that, as the power of the landowner passed into the hands of the new adventurers, they – the men and women from the farms and

22

cottages – would become a new phenomenon – a working class – which would shake the established order to its roots?

Accordingly, the stripping and recasting of the Torrs began, a process in which New Mills would become both homestead and workplace not only to farmers, coal miners, spinners and cottage weavers, but to papermakers, stonemasons and quarrymen; bleachers, dyers, engravers and potters; iron, rope, brass and chemical workers; builders, engineers, mechanics; bargees and railwaymen; and to a growing horde of shopkeepers, bankers and undertakers; of poor men, beggarmen, thieves.

They came from the fields and moors, from hamlets near and far, and even from distant towns, not by the hundreds perhaps, but by the score. They converged on the gorge where unfriendly, cacophonous, beyond-human-scale noises filled the air. In the mills they faced long hours, paltry wages, and wretched and dangerous conditions where fire was a constant threat. They were known, not as men and women, but as 'hands'. Children as young as six were casually exploited by mill owners and managers who rode roughshod over the perfunctory regulations designed to protect them.

As the 19th century approached there were no fewer than seven mills in and near the gorge – Salem, Beard, Barnes, Torr, Rock, Torr Vale and Grove. Yet for many of the mill owners the revolution had not begun auspiciously. There were disappointments and setbacks; many changes in ownership, occupation and strategy. Even occasional catastrophes.

But there is no holding back. Industrial

The Peak Forest Canal.

Church Road Bridge looking towards the Midland Railway viaduct.

initiatives continue to intensify. Houses begin to spread along the present High Street from Salem Bridge and, to meet the needs of in-comers, clusters of terraced cottages – four or five storeys down slope, two upslope – will be crushed together on the steep, precarious hillsides, hillsides which will become known as Bamford, Spout Gutter, Brookside and Redgate. Across the valley the Peak Forest Canal will open up new sites for industrial development in Warksmoor and beyond.

Yet, New Mills' ambitions will be thwarted by the valley of the Torrs. Wrapping itself round Torr Top like a mediaeval moat it will be regarded as a deterrent to movement and expansion. It must, at all costs, be spanned.

The Church Road bridge, a critical link in the Thornsett to Warksmoor chain, crossed the upper limb of the gorge in 1835. (Its strange low-lying buttress arches which today give it an unusual 'double deck' profile, were added to the original structure when faults appeared in the bridge's fabric after 50 years of service.) The bridge, however, was of little practical use to New Mills. For what the town needed was a north-south link from Torr Top over the gorge.

The Union Road bridge – though not for many a year – would solve the problem. Rising 90 feet from the valley floor – its stonework as clean-cut and exact today as it ever was – the bridge leaps across the gorge in four graceful arches, the northernmost of which springs directly from the rock face. Restrained and meticulously proportioned, the Union Road bridge is made from stone hewn from the Torrs themselves. Standing a little down river at right angles to its rugged east-west neighbour, it would be opened in 1884 in a grand ceremony to which we shall return later.

The New Mills Old Prize Band. (All items courtesy of Anne and Ian Mason)

The New Mills Old Prize Band

The Battle of Waterloo was yet to be fought when (according to an unidentified newspaper report of 1912) Timothy Beard gathered together his 'goodly company of rural musicians' and founded the New Mills Old Prize Band. That was in 1812 and – although Stalybridge might beg to differ – the band would be the first of its kind in the world.

Imagine those musicians stepping out along the streets in their 'tall grey hats, blue swallow-tail tunics, epaulettes and red-

Christmas 2002, on the Market Street promenade.

striped trousers'. What a sensation! And how they must have 'uplifted many a heart weighed down with the [unshed] burdens of the Napoleonic Wars'.

One hundred years later, a grand open-air festival was planned to mark

The band in May 1999.

the band's glorious centenary. Unfavourable weather conditions, however, dictated that celebrations be moved indoors, into the Town Hall – a splendid venue, but one quite unable to cope with

To Mr Pollit:
Dear Sir,

I am instructed by our committee to say that they accept your offer of £3 0 0 for playing in procession on the occasion of the visit of the Duke…

John Wood
Hon Sec.

the large numbers of people eager to attend. In fact – although distinguished 'gentry of the district' were comfortably accommodated – the musicians themselves were less fortunate, and were forced to 'play their selections outside, the windows of the Town Hall being opened.'

At the beginning of World War One the band enlisted en masse and sadly, as hostilities dragged on, lost nine of their number. Yet in 1919 – defiant, applauded – they marched once again through the streets of New Mills. As indeed they did in 1945, and have done ever since. From carnivals and concerts to thanksgiving and remembrance, from Low Leighton and Newtown, to Alsfeld and Eudorf, the Prize Band has served the community well.

A generous Lottery grant, Co-operative sponsorship (it is now know as The United Norwest Co-op Band), a busy schedule under their conductor Jim Farnsworth, and continuing public affection, should enable the Oldest Prize Band in the World to approach its double century with confidence.

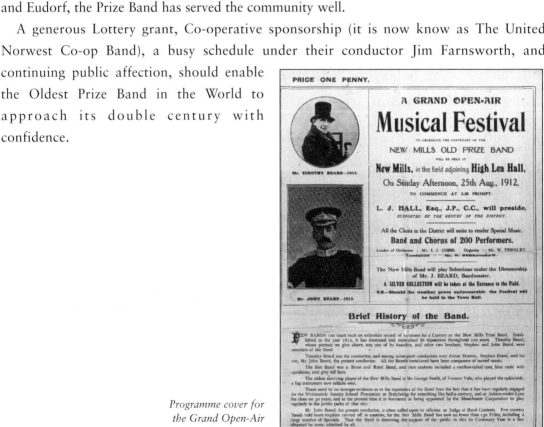

Programme cover for the Grand Open-Air Music Festival of August 1912.

Macclesfield, 1981.

An early photograph of the New Mills Old Prize Band.

Street scenes ... past and present

A deserted Market Street. (Courtesy John Hemsworth)

The former George Hotel from Meal Street.

Market Street on a busy Saturday afternoon.

High Street, Livesley's and the George Hotel. (Courtesy John Hemsworth)

Union Road.

Market Street panorama. (Photo © Gary C. Wood, 2003)

Harris the tailors on High Street. The Dog and Partridge is on the extreme left. (Courtesy John Hemsworth)

St Mary's Road. (Courtesy John Hemsworth)

Birch Vale Terrace, built in 1870, on Sycamore Road. (Courtesy John Hemsworth)

Thornsett, looking towards Sitch Lane, in the early years of the 20th century. (Courtesy John Hemsworth)

Bridge Street. The fine houses of Spring Bank can be seen in the background. (Courtesy John Hemsworth)

Market Street. (Courtesy Evelyn Hulse)

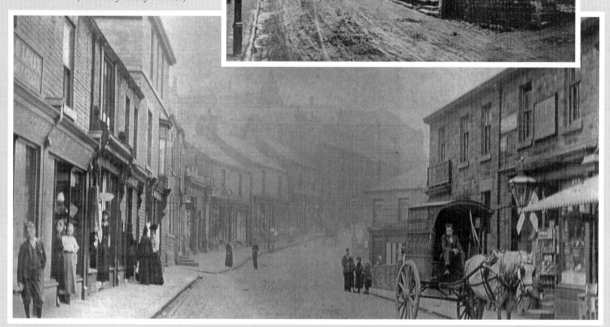

Chapter 2
A Mixed Harvest

On the vexed question of turnpike tolls, for instance, while in the press urbane discussion generally flourishes, on the streets themselves the lawless behaviour of roving mobs threatens to undo the very gains of civilisation.

Chaos is abroad! Constables are stoned, tollbooth attendants beaten, tollgates uprooted and thrown into the river, suspected attackers cast into jail. Mysterious effigies are flourished and savaged,

T HE 1820s and 30s yielded a very mixed harvest in the 'romantically picturesque and beautiful' region of New Mills. Several of her industrial concerns – whether through fire, recession, bad management or unprofitable practice – had been forced to close, while others were struggling to overcome earlier misfortunes of one kind or another, or were languishing in a limbo of inaction. Mill workers had been thrown onto the streets and were forced to scrape a living, and often barely that, in any way they could.

The prospect of the establishment of a Poor Law workhouse at Low Leighton added to a general sense of disquiet, as did the perceived injustice regarding turnpike tolls, and the belief that perhaps the poor and dispossessed of the town were increasingly taking matters into their own hands.

St George's Works.

Two views of the Albion Road toll booth, scene of many serious disturbances. (Courtesy John Hemsworth)

and hundreds of people – some dressed as women to divert suspicion – gather to storm the tollbooths. The courts are bustling and the turnpike commissioners, not knowing which way to jump, at one moment scream for their pound of flesh, and at another counsel discretion and conciliation.

Political clashes of a broader kind – especially in 1837, General Election year – are exacerbated by the so called 'banditti' of New Mills, who threaten to bludgeon all who oppose them; and following the People's Charter of 1838, guns are on sale at a local beer house, and Chartist gangs take to roaming the streets and alleys of our 'improving city of mirthful jollity'.

Salem Mill. (Courtesy John Hemsworth)

Yet despite these amazing events, New Mills actually did enjoy a fair share of mirth and jollity, and of ordinary everyday situations. People went about their business, children played hopping games, couples went a-courtin' and got married; fields were ploughed, bread was baked, vegetables peeled, boots repaired, babies fed. And once in a while great events were celebrated. Events such as the Coronation, in the high summer of 1838, of young Queen Victoria.

New Mills, bless her heart, is determined to fling wide the gates and blow the trumpets. In a flurry of patriotic excitement faces are scrubbed, musical instruments polished, houses and shops decked with banners and bunting, Union Jacks hoisted. There are parties, entertainments and parades, and a wonderful celebration is held especially for the children of the town, all 1,250 of them, 'clean, healthy and respectable in appearance'.

Of the proprietors of industry who arrange Coronation treats for their employees, few are as generous as John Potts of St George's Works. Mr Potts – an internationally famous engraver – himself leads the festivities. His factory is elaborately decorated, cannons are fired, flags raised, and a splendid meal of roast beef and plum pudding is washed down with lashings of good old English ale. Later, everyone joins in a chorus of patriotic song and Mr Potts, 'surrounded by the joyful faces of his workmen', proposes the loyal toast. It is an occasion to savour.

–oOo–

At the beginning of the 1840s, one might be inclined to think of New Mills as an extensive town with a large population. But this would actually be far from true. There had of course been considerable growth since the opening of the century when the records (in 1801), had documented a grand total of 1,787 inhabitants, but in fact the population had reached only three and a half thousand – 3,595 to be precise – by 1841.

As for the ground plan of New Mills, the Tithe Map published in that year shows it to be a long,

The Wesleyan Chapel, St George's Road. (Courtesy John Hemsworth)

thin wedge of a place, stretching from Sam Goddard's White Hart Inn in the north to Torr Top in the south, and from the River Sett (or River Kinder as it appears on the map) in the east, to the newly completed Spring Bank (and Market Street) in the west. Apart from Salem (or Bower) Mill, and a small clutch of buildings – including the Wesleyan Chapel, St George's Works and Chadwick's Bleachworks in the fold of Hyde Bank and Church Lane – there is practically nothing but meadowland east of the river. The town, then, is less than half a mile long and, at its widest point, not quite 200 yards across – a tiny cramped stage which inevitably magnified the affairs of its players.

It is perhaps worth closer inspection. Let us imagine, then, coming in to New Mills from Mellor in 1841. As we drive down the hill we first

pass the Independents Chapel, and come almost immediately to the White Hart Inn.

We may now choose to pass through the town (towards Torr Top) via any of three routes: the high road, the low road, or an 'even lower' road (not to be confused with the lowest road of all, which would lead us down the difficult setted tracks and into the gorge!).

The high road – Spring Bank – is bright and new, and is delightfully open to the elements. It is a fresh and breezy ride. To our left the land dips away out of sight, while to our right only two small knots of cottages and the Warrenites Chapel stand between us and the empty windswept meadows – Top o' th' Bank, New Meadow, Scotch Piece and Tenter Hill – that stretch westwards as if to infinity.

The low road is quite a different story. It's a

mishmash of smells, noise and bustle. This route will take us down Dye House Lane past Quarmby's engraving shop on the left. To the right are the town's lock-up, George Pearson's smithy, and three lively inns – the Cock, the Grapes and, as we enter High Street, the Bull's Head (run by Jim Etchells). Carrying on we pass Coates's butchers shop, the Wesleyan chapel and schoolroom, and Garratt's beer house, before coming to another rowdy trio of inns – the George, Martha Hibbert's Masons Arms and Joe Waterhouse's Dog and Partridge. All in all, with the inns, the beer houses and the good company, it must have been some challenge to remain uninfluenced by the evils of alcohol in this part of the town.

And now, the even lower road. This route, rather less unruly it must be said, once again takes us down Dye House Lane and then to the bottom part of High Street. But now, at McRae's, we fork to the left and on to Meal Street. From here we can see – again to our left – some of the closely packed Torrs cottages tumbling away down the hillside and, below them, James Sidebottom's works – Beard Mill rambling down to the river.

All three of these routes converge at the Crown Inn, recently built by Richard Bennett at the top end of Market Street.

As for the southern part of town, the triangle formed by Market Street, Rock Street and Torr Top Street, is both filled and flanked with cottages and small yards. There is also a foundry, a smithy and some stables. The foot of Market Street, where one day Union Road will begin, sweeps around Mr Bennett's meadow and joins the road to Hague Bar and Marple.

This then, is the extent of New Mills in 1841: a concentration of a few hundred houses and cottages, a score of shops, a dozen mills, a few

St George's Church. (Photo © Gary C. Wood, 2003)

chapels, a scattering of small businesses and eight inns. And oh yes, far to the east, near Marsh Lane Head, standing in glorious isolation as if, as someone wrote, 'awaiting the town's arrival', the handsome St George's Church.

–oOo–

And so we come to the building of Union Road and its magnificent bridge. But I must warn you, it is a long and convoluted process!

In 1806 the first of the turnpike roads to affect New Mills – the road from Marple – had cut across the northern portion of Torr Top. Thirty years later the Thornsett turnpike had passed the town to the south. In the 1840s this arrangement continued to determine communications. As mobility advanced, however, it was clear that if freer patterns of movement were to be introduced, a link between these two roads was crucial. By now the old tracks and bridges in the gorge itself were very dangerous, and the only practicable route for traffic to Warksmoor was the long and circuitous one via Salem Bridge. A connecting road – from north to south across Torr Top – was an obvious solution, but this would require a quite monumental and expensive bridge to be built across the Goyt from the southern rim of the Torrs.

In 1844 the first New Mills parish council – formed, as we have said, from the alliance of Ollersett, Beard, Whitle and Thornsett – held its inaugural meeting. Although the parish officers may have had the will to tackle the bridge issue, it soon became evident that progress would not be easy. A plethora of antiquated rules, rights and regulations, not to mention a range of modern questions, created a tangle of red tape which tightly bound the hands which might otherwise have done the deed, and it was plain almost from the outset that the officers could barely wiggle their fingers, much less accomplish the sweeping gestures such a grand scheme would have necessitated. And so, the project lay on the table… for the next 30 years!

When, however, a man stumbled to his death in 1875 attempting to cross the gorge on foot, the coroner was moved to comment in his report that New Mills maintained 'some of the most wretched and miserable roads' imaginable, that 'a local authority ought at once to be formed' and that its first business 'should be the construction of proper roads from one part of the town to the other'.

A year later a petition made by ratepayers to the newly-elected Urban Sanitary Authority drew attention to a clear need for 'union' between New Mills (in Derbyshire), and the rising locality known as Newtown (in Cheshire). Such entreaties, however, did not necessarily find favour among the inhabitants of Newtown – or at least the more militant of them. Why should they – with fine roads, a busy railway, a thriving canal and modern steam-powered mills – why should they agree to further links with New Mills with its jaded amenities and crumbling infrastructure? Why on earth should they subsidise such a place? Surely the best policy would be to keep one's distance!

In any event it was not only a question of finance. Pride was at stake! After all, until recently Newtown had been known by its original name, Warksmoor. The change to a more forward-looking name embraced all of the ambition of this independent and confident community.

Nonetheless, perhaps inevitably, the economic value of improved communication was eventually

Union Road Bridge, during construction in 1884. (Courtesy Town Hall)

recognised, and when, in due course, the Authority put forward a number of schemes for the betterment of the area, the Union Road Bridge project was among them. The consequent demolition of Torr Top Hall, and the dislocation of Richard Bennett's estate, were narrowly approved and Mr Storey, the engineer, and Mr Walmsey, the contractor, were duly appointed to initiate an enterprise which would, on its completion, lead to radical changes not only for New Mills and Newtown, but for places far beyond.

The opening of the High Level Bridge, New Mills, on Saturday 7 June 1884 was – as the extensive schedule of celebrants would affirm – one of the greatest events in the town's history. Those taking part were to include the members of the Local Board and Committee, Gentry and Tradesmen; the National School, the Wesleyan and Independent Schools, the United Methodist Free Church and Primitive Methodist Schools; the Oddfellows, Foresters, Shepherds and Sons of Temperance Societies; and – appearing on Lurries and Drays – Trades and Manufacturers. The procession would start at 12 o'clock, headed by the Salford Borough Reed Band, while the Audenshaw Temperance Prize Band and the Hayfield Brass Band would lead the parades of schools.

The Union Road Bridge and the road itself not only established the desired link between north and south, but in so doing defined the ground plan of modern New Mills. Little by little, buildings – of which John Wharmby's Jubilee Buildings was the first – began to line the new road and, as time passed, Torr Top exchanged its scrub and meadowland for the trappings – domestic, commercial and public – of a lively late-Victorian town.

Thornsett Band outside Aspenshaw Hall in 1910. (Courtesy New Mills Library)

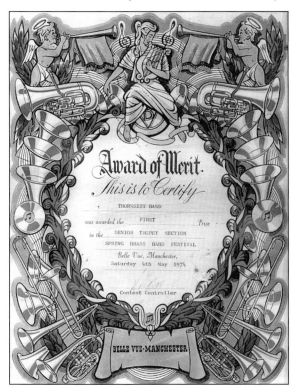

The Award of Merit, 1974. (Courtesy Thornsett Band)

The 'Smiling Morn' Band

The children would hear it first: a scattering of sounds carried to and fro on the breeze; a fragment of melody; a bass drum's isolated thuds. 'Here they come,' they would shout. Then, as the music took shape, people would gather on doorsteps to cheer the bandsmen as they made their way to Birch Vale station. It was Whitsuntide, so they were expected. And, as they marched – bound for Stalybridge and Ashton Walks – they would play *Hail Smiling Morn*. For 80 years Thornsett musicians, their children and grand-children, would make this same journey.

Along the river Tame they would be known as the 'Smiling Morn' band, but

this would not be their only nickname. For William Halliwell, their celebrated conductor of the 1930s, would affectionately refer to them as his 'Jewel in the hills'. It all sounds very romantic!

But, of course, there were good times and bad. Established in 1876, Thornsett Band had enjoyed a period of excellence in the 1930s which was quite unequalled in the following decades, and it was not until Brian Taylor became conductor in the 1960s that the band re-emerged as a force to be reckoned with. In 1967 they won the Junior Shield at Belle Vue, and in so doing anticipated a succession of triumphs which culminated in a famous 3rd Section National Championships victory in 1974, and the East Midlands 2nd Section Championships in the 1980s. In the same decade, however, some of the band's most experienced players departed, and so began a new phase in Thornsett's chequered history.

The band hut. (Courtesy Evelyn Hulse)

Young players were brought in from local schools and, under the guidance of David Ford and Maurice Hallam, a youth band was formed – a band which became, in 2001, the official Thornsett Band.

Since then, a lottery grant, the services of conductor Gary Parker, and renewed enthusiasm have hopefully prepared the band for many a smiling morn to come.

The champion band of Great Britain, 1974. (Photos courtesy Thornsett Band)

Thornsett Band, 1912.

Time Gentlemen Please!

Hare and Hounds, Low Leighton, 27 January 1940. (Courtesy Evelyn Hulse)

The Mason's Arms. (Courtesy Evelyn Hulse)

The Hare and Hounds, 2003.

The Pack Horse Inn.

The Old New Inn,
Thornsett.

The New Inn. (Courtesy John Hemsworth)

The Royal Oak.

The Crown (now the Torrs) on Market Street.

The White Hart Inn.

Chapter 3
Theatre of Affection

The Manchester & County Bank, High Street.

The Midland Railway Viaduct of 1902.

J UST as water power had carried New Mills into the first half of the 19th century, steam would drive her into the second. In the new factories steam would rule the roost, while on the railways it would revolutionise mobility.

Yet the initial phase of railway mania which had affected many parts of England in the 1840s had come and gone long before the first steam train pulled into Newtown station in 1857. In the 1840s flurry of speculation it had been almost inevitable that many companies – given their investments in often rash enterprises – would overreach themselves. Add to that a national economic slump in the late 1840s, and it was little wonder that in some cases the railway experience ended in bankruptcy and even dishonour. Accordingly, for 10 years reticence outweighed ambition and projects dwindled. But in the 1850s, with an improvement in economic conditions and

Albion Mill.

line which ran from Stockport to Whaley Bridge and which would later be extended to Buxton and to Manchester.

To the north of the gap, although much later, another railway would sweep in from Manchester and Marple, and would arrive at New Mills Central – a station perched on a rocky, wooded sill immediately above the Torrs gorge. Central Station opened in 1865 and is today still noted for its fine stationmaster's house, and other original buildings. But in order to continue eastwards to link up with the Derby railway, the Marple line would have to negotiate a high embankment, sheer above the gorge, burrow under Torr Top, and emerge from the Torrs directly onto a viaduct over the River Sett! These Victorian engineers, however, both clever and stern of spirit, were not to be denied, and the Derby extension opened in 1867, to be followed by the final stretch to Sheffield in 1894.

In between the north and south railways, a third – a direct route to Manchester – was later built across the flood plain itself. Branching off from the Sheffield line, it positively soars above the valley on the striking 13-arch viaduct of 1902. Almost immediately, however, it disappears, somewhat unceremoniously, beneath the streets of Newtown.

As a matter of fact tunnels, viaducts, embankments and cuttings feature prominently in railway engineering around New Mills. Stand on the platform of Central Station for instance, and one can see two dark tunnel entrances penetrating the rock face of Torr Top – the one to the right providing for the Sheffield line, the one to the left, now disused, carrying what was the New Mills–Hayfield railway of 1868. This once important line – now the Sett Valley trail – passed,

a recovery in confidence, a second exuberant wave of railway building began.

Although in many respects the New Mills region was topographically discouraging to the railway adventurers, it did have one priceless asset: the so-called River Goyt gap – an area of relatively flat land between the Pennine hills – a gateway to the great industrial city of Manchester. To the south of that gap the gentler slopes had long been claimed by the Peak Forest Canal and the Disley turnpike, but not to be deterred by overcrowding, the railway makers went ahead anyway and built a line along the same route – a

Birch Vale Printworks. (Courtesy John Hemsworth)

Manor Bank Cottages, built in the 1890s on Hyde Bank Road. (Courtesy John Hemsworth)

The grotto at St Mary's.

St Mary's Church.

on its journey, Watford Bridge Printworks, the old Bate Mill Bleachworks, Garrison Bleachworks and Birch Vale Printworks. In its early days it was indispensable to these factories, and at its peak handled 18 trains a day to Manchester.

–oOo–

Newtown was something of a focus for the steam age. It could boast modern factories standing in spacious surroundings – factories powered by steam engines, convenient of access on the banks of the Peak Forest Canal, and close to the turnpike roads; forward-looking companies exuding superiority over their water-prescribed forerunners. Five new mills outflanked the five ancient mills of the Torrs: Warksmoor Mill, 1850; Albion, 1859; Victoria, 1860; Brunswick, 1872; and Woodside, also 1872.

In the meantime the older mills had been huffing and puffing, with varying degrees of success, to keep up: Torr had introduced a steam engine, together with a tall chimney to carry smoke out of the gorge, in 1846. Torr Vale installed a steam engine of her own in 1856. Rock

The Co-operative Building on
High Street.

(Left) The Hall Street
Constabulary.

The old Board School on
Spring Bank.

New Mills Town Hall. (Photo © Gary C. Wood, 2003)

Mill had chopped and changed roles – from calico printing to paper manufacture – while Barnes was lying in a state of dilapidation, and Hyde Bank – steam engine, water wheel and all – was, in 1886, up for auction.

Other local mills too – half a dozen on the River Sett together with St George's Works and Grove Mill – spent the second half of the 19th century veering between good times and bad. Industry was forever a theatre of wanton contrasts: of alternating full and short time employment; of intervals of wellbeing which would lift the spirits of the whole town; of curious events and practices such as the reported slaughter of cows (from Middle Cliff Farm) to pay the employees of Birch Vale Printworks 'partly in beef'; of savage blazes, such as that which destroyed the cotton waste mill at St George's Works; of sudden closures, and of optimistic revivals such as Joseph Stafford's purchase of the somewhat uncertain Bower Mill in 1853, and the building of the mill cottages (called Salem) in 1856.

And in truth, for all their steam-powered optimism, the story was not dissimilar in Newtown. For nothing – not enlightened ownership and philanthropic management, not modern energy sources and machinery, not up-to-the-minute delivery and distribution programmes by road, rail and canal – nothing could resist cotton famine, fire and economic vacillation.

–oOo–

Yet for all the social and economic fluctuations that beset her evolution, New Mills – between

1850 and 1900 – continues to acquire the amenities, institutions, buildings and personalities of a dynamic community. She becomes, as it were, a theatre of affection, active in every mood. Though not in a spectacular way, her population continues to rise – from a little under 4,500 in 1851, to 6,000 at the turn of the century – and at the same time she adopts many of the physical aspects of her modern configuration, including several buildings familiar to those who are acquainted with the New Mills of today.

And, should we not know her buildings, what would we predict for them? What would be their likely characteristics? Solidity, confidence, assurance and – even allowing for an occasional flourish of Victorian ornamentation – restraint. The buildings of New Mills display few, if any, flights of artistic fancy. There are no shocks, little or no rhetoric, no explosions of colour, and little variety of materials. None of the ostentation for which the Victorian age was noted.

Her churches, with the possible exception of St George's, are modest of aspiration, and even the fine mill owners' houses – High Lee Hall and its like, and the 'middle class' developments, such as those on the rise behind Spring Bank – appear to 'know their place', and are in no way disproportionate to the scale of the town, or the landscapes round about.

Of those varying heights and levels, which

St James's Church.

generally create the visual energy in a town's profile, there are many, but in New Mills' case they have nothing to do with architectural extravagance or audacity. They are simply topographical. Here, it is the rise and fall of the land that dramatises the buildings and not vice versa. In fact in their scale, proportion, colour, texture and conviction, the buildings of New Mills could hardly be more consonant.

Just look at the splendid doorway of the Manchester and County Bank in High Street. Would it not have enticed you to place your financial affairs in the hands of its denizens? Or consider the Co-operative building beside the Town Hall, or the indoor market next to the Crown Inn (or The Torrs as it is now known). Who could possibly deny the probity of people who worked in such settings, or could waver as regards the wholesomeness of their provisions? Who could have doubted the integrity of the bobby who manned the Hall Street constabulary, or could have questioned the quality of spiritual guidance and comfort one would have found within the portals of the Methodist Free church in High Street? Are not the buildings of New Mills a telling outward manifestation of a people to whom John Wesley referred as 'earnest, artless and loving'? And see how the Board School on Spring Bank (and, in its subtler way, Mr Widdows' handsome Grammar School on Church Lane) see how they radiate knowledge and understanding, not to say wisdom.

And regard the Town Hall itself – grand, but not too grand; raised high on its hill above the hoi polloi, but not too high. Who could have hesitated to trust officers who served in such an edifice? Even the Masonic Hall and the Conservative Club – should you have felt drawn to the callings they

The John Mackie Memorial Fountain. (Photo © Gary C. Wood, 2003)

represent – would surely have confirmed your beliefs, and endorsed your prejudices.

This is an architecture making an art of non-intimidation; a familiar, revivalist style, classical, safe and sound; an architecture whose very body language assuages fears and anxieties, and quickens confidence. These buildings are not exactly cosy, not precisely inviting, but they are sure and serious and pious, and, believe me, you can trust them.

–oOo–

But of course buildings do not actually constitute a community. As a matter of fact the very best they can do is bear witness to the ways, needs, beliefs and deeds of the people who plan, erect and use them.

The New Mills Bowls, Cricket and Tennis Club

1996 DC&C league champions. (All items courtesy Geoff Griffiths)

The retirement of Fred Lee. Mr Lee (left) and Geoff Griffiths.

New Mills Cricket Club had been a thriving concern 'for generations' when, in the spring of 1901, it met its match in the mighty Midland Railway Company. More discreet than valiant – for who could compete with a new railway line? – its members were forced to abandon the Albion Road Riverside Ground which for so long had staged their contests. Whether or not the clubs' bowls and tennis sections existed at the time history does not tell us, but whatever the case, all seemed lost.

Until that is – according to the *Ashton Reporter* of 11 May 1901 – a number of public spirited gentlemen stepped into the breach, formed a limited company (which has survived to this day), and acquired a 20-year lease on an excellent plot beside Church Road. Soon the new ground, laid out by Scattergood and Warrington, was enhanced by 'a beautiful pavilion' – designed by Mr Bowden of Hayfield and built by Mr Swindells of New Mills – 'the pretty appearance' of which 'excited general admiration, and both architect and contractor were in receipt of numerous congratulations.'

On 4 May 1901, an opening ceremony – which had included the inauguration of the bowling green – had been attended by 1,500 people, the only shadow upon the day being the defeat of New Mills in the ensuing celebratory cricket match: 'New Mills 73, Hayfield 117, all the batters of each side being got out.'

During 42 seasons (from 1909) in the High Peak League, New Mills enjoyed many notable successes including – to name but a handful – five cup and three league championships in the 1930s; while in the 1950s, having joined the new Derbyshire & Cheshire League, New Mills achieved a hat-trick of championships: 1953, 1954 and 1955.

A club record.

Of great occasions there have been many and, over the years, some of cricket's most distinguished players (Hobbs, Sutcliffe, Constantine, Mike Hendrick, Bob Taylor, Mike Atherton) have appeared at Church Road. With the refurbishment and extension of the pavilion (thanks to Sport England and the Derbyshire Environmental Trust, among others), the New Mills Bowling, Cricket and Tennis Club has begun the new millennium on a supremely positive note.

1977 – Royal Silver Jubilee year.

Edward Godward, 1841–1908. (Courtesy NMLHS)

People like Edward Godward, Quaker, Yorkshireman, mill owner, so called 'benevolent autocrat', who – given his passionate interests in industry, commerce, politics, religion, education and, yes architecture – seems to have a finger in every pie. It is Mr Godward who, in the early 1860s, while proprietor of Brunswick Mill, is smitten by the ideals embodied in the recently established New Mills Equitable Co-operative and Industrial Society, and becomes a leading light in its promotion. The 'Co-op' – notwithstanding its window boxes and pink curtains, its polite servers in jackets and white aprons, and its convenient opening hours (including a late night until 11pm on Saturdays) – is not simply about a pleasant shopping experience. It is, in its Victorian way, about community, self-improvement, investment, education, temperance and good citizenship – matters close to Mr Godward's philanthropic heart. It is a strange compound of commerce and profit, prudence and morality; an organisation favouring abstinence, yet selling British wines at 1s 5d a bottle, providing mortgages and loans, holding tea parties and magic lantern shows, inaugurating evening classes in the Navvies Preaching Room, re-establishing the Band of Hope, paying student fees for the children of members, and subscribing to hospitals. The Society opens new branches whenever it can do so, and even expands from retail into cotton manufacturing – an area in which Mr Godward's experience and expertise as a master of industry can be profitably employed. In fact Mr Godward is instrumental in many initiatives, including the construction and supervision of the new Co-operative store on the corner of High Street, and especially the propagation of the Society's principles and philosophies.

Ever onward and upward, the aptly-named Mr Godward – a more than typically virile member of the new, largely self-made, socially responsible middle class – is so energetic that he can by no means be contained by the Co-operative movement alone. He personally designs not only his own home – Cliff House in Albion Road – but the Board Schools at Hague Bar, Newtown, Thornsett and New Mills itself. He bequeaths a scholarship to the new Church Road School, becomes chairman of the Local Board and, in 1894 – to cap a brilliant career – becomes the first chairman of the New Mills Urban District Council.

Edward Godward, a tireless worker for the community, a Liberal with strong and often contentious opinions, is so highly regarded by his peers that when he dies in 1908, his funeral procession is three quarters of a mile long. He is laid to rest at the Friends' burial ground in Low Leighton, on 3 June.

Mr Godward's funeral procession. (Courtesy Evelyn Hulse)

Many such residents, via endowments and good works, devote much of their lives to elevating, educating and refining the community. Sometimes – as is the case with the Mackies – their names are quite literally inscribed into the very stone of the buildings that affirm their efforts.

John Mackie – 'a good man and a just' – holds important positions with the School Board and with the Mechanics' Institute, and together with his wife Mary Elizabeth – daughter of the Inghams of Watford Printworks – commissions St James's Church and its six picturesque almshouses, in memory of his wife's parents. Mr Mackie is seemingly never too high and mighty nor too busy for real involvement in the community. He arranges certificates and prizes for school children and, on the occasion of Queen Victoria's Golden Jubilee, he prepares a treat for the pupils of Thornsett, 'tea and buns in the school room' together with 'a medal and a book – the Life of the Queen'. Mrs Mackie, too, is most energetic and after her husband's death endows the Memorial Library in the New Mills School of Science to honour his enlightened deeds.

James Hibbert, another of the town's champions, gives much of his time to improving educational facilities and religious institutions. He helps establish the Mechanics' Institute, agitates for the foundation of a secondary school, argues vigorously for the building of a town hall, and contributes handsomely to the installation therein of a free library.

As New Mills approaches the 20th century, she does so with her formal structures and practices firmly in place. The officers of the Urban District Council have resolutely taken up their positions in the principal chamber of the public hall (which, incidentally, will not be referred to as the Town Hall until 1899). In the same building a quarterly County Court is held under the direction of registrar Richard Brown and distinguished judge W.C. Smyly; while on every fourth Wednesday at 10.30am, Petty Sessions take place. On Saturdays, between 5 and 7pm the Savings Bank is open, and on Mondays, between 7.45 and 8.45pm, one may invest in the Economical Permanent Building Society.

And we should not forget the School Board, an imposing body of gentlemen which convenes at the Board School on Spring Bank, with Mr Hibbert in the chair, and Mr Godward as clerk, on the last Tuesday in each month.

The Friends' Meeting House at Low Leighton.

James Hibbert, 1831–1905

A few pages from Mr Hibbert's six-volume, leather-bound *Reminiscences connected with the progress and history of NEW MILLS.*

Fern Bank garden. Miss Hibbert and Mr Hibbert, 3 September 1900, among the roses and dahlias. (All items courtesy Town Hall)

A page of James Hibbert's handwriting.

Fern Bank House.

New Mills parish magazine, November 1898.

St George's Church bells

In 1898 James Hibbert – though strongly nonconformist – presented St George's Anglican Church with a peal of six bells. The octave was completed in 1901 with Mr Hibbert's presentation of the two bells pictured here.

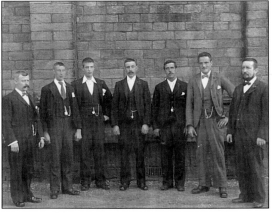

The original bell-ringers.

Chapter 4
Images

IT MUST be most gratifying to hold a significant community voice, to have one's name carved in stone or displayed on ornamental fountains or illuminated plaques, or for one's accomplishments to be celebrated in great set pieces of public respect. And it is not to be suggested that the men (and occasionally women) of New Mills who gained such recognition did so without just cause. But it goes without saying that most people who make up a community do so without having achieved important civic positions, without acquiring huge sums of money and without indulging in high-profile ventures. For by and large, it is the workers, tradespeople and small-time professionals – those who provide goods and services, hopefully for a decent profit – who perhaps do most to establish and maintain the viability of a growing town. The New Mills directory of 1896 lists no fewer than 250 of these 'bread and butter' people, among them the following: Jonathan Arnfield of Spring Bank, an importer of yeast, Benjamin Cooper of Union Road, a pork butcher, and James Lockwood, a saddler of Market Street; Catherine Courtney, a school mistress at St Mary's, Henry Barber, a bank manager, Joseph Clarke, station master, William Bates, music teacher, and William Lowe, rate collector.

And there is Thomas Turner, the proprietor of the old curiosity shop on Torr Top Street, and James Richardson who keeps the toy shop on High Street. George Chadwick of Market Street dresses tripe, Ester Howes creates delicacies for her confectioners shop in Bridge Street, Thomas Rigby runs a hat shop on High Street, and Elizabeth Arnfield has a dressmaking business near Ester Howes' confectioners.

For high-quality coal you may depend on Joseph Walton, for watch repairs Isaac Goodwin-Jackson, for books, William Leigh, and for fancy goods of all descriptions, George Walker. Jas Green on High Street will provide your fruit and veg, and will also lend you money; John Lomas will cobble your boots, Margaret Smith will furnish your house, while Emma Simmister can offer a good range of curtain and other materials.

Bodily health may be entrusted to Alfred Livesley or John Byrne the chemists, to Leah Roberts the herbalist, or, on more serious matters, to Charles Grindrod the surgeon. Incidentally, if ever you should require a piano tuner William Whitehead of Spring Bank is highly recommended, or if you would like, perhaps, to sit for a romantic family photograph, James Randles can boast all of the latest equipment at his Bridge Street studio. If, however, your finances are low why not visit Joseph Johnson, your friendly pawnbroker? Of course for more major issues, financial or otherwise legal, you may have to call upon Charles Jowett, the solicitor, to defend your interests. Failing all else, by the way, you can drown your sorrows in one (or more) of 20 hotels, inns and taverns in the vicinity.

At which point, for fear of over-indulgence, we shall pause. But not without mentioning all of the remaining townsfolk of New Mills – the majority in fact – those men, women and children with no names to recall, and about whom there is nothing to write except that without them there would be no town at all.

–oOo–

In the annals of a town's history certain stories are told again and again. In the case of New Mills one such story is that of the infamous drunkard and poacher, Thomas Handford. It is known as 'The Drunkard's Reform'.

Handford, in persistently falling foul of the law, had often found himself incarcerated in the town's prison in Dye House Lane. One day, however, having witnessed a drinking partner drop down dead in the Cock Inn, Handford resolved to turn his back on the demon drink forever. Some time later, in a deed heavily symbolic, he purchased the

prison, converted it into a cottage, and lived there until his death.

On 25 March 1899, the *Sunday Companion*, a highly respectable and temperate newspaper, published the story of Handford's 'remarkable teetotal conversion' as an example to all, and printed a photograph of his widow standing in the doorway of their prison home. For many years a carved stone plaque celebrated this heart-warming reformation, and even today a replica of the original plaque can be found attached to the cottage wall.

The Drunkard's Reform. Thomas Handford's widow in the cottage doorway. Hands clasped. Mesmeric. (Courtesy NMLHS)

So, there it is. The tale has been told once more! Yet what brings it to life are not the bare bones of its telling, but the photograph. The mesmeric image of that figure – Handford's widow – standing in the shadows of the cottage doorway, hands clasped together.

Union Road c.1910 and the black smoke of Torr Mill chimney. (Courtesy NMLHS)

It was around this time that photography, though not new, began to affect popular imagination, and the irresistible love affair with the camera began.

Newtown Wesleyans at the Band of Hope Gala, on 10 August 1912. (Courtesy NMLHS)

Suddenly, in photographs of the time, New Mills draws breath, and today, one hundred and more years later, we can share in the images of the town and its people. Monochromatic visions. Ashen, greyish or perhaps sepia images of cobbled streets and alleys. Sunlight very nearly as sombre as shadow. Mists hanging over shops and terraces. Black smoke billowing from mill chimneys. And the men and women and children of New Mills, gazing at the eye of the camera with inquisitive, smiling, surprised, bewildered or deadpan faces.

Posing casually or proudly, or being caught unawares. Top hatted, neatly suited, aproned, black stockinged or deeply skirted. Uniformed, costumed, capped or bonneted. Standing, hands on hips, walking, driving carts, opening doors, riding bicycles, shopping. Peeping infants clinging to mothers' hands. Perky babies bolt upright in penny farthing prams.

Here they are, some of the very people we may have named a couple of pages back. The staff of

New Mills railway station, shopkeepers posing before their wonderful window displays, the pretty girls of the Band of Hope gala, morris dancers in sashes and clogs. Here is Edward Godward's funeral cortège, a likeness of James Hibbert, and George Walker himself on the step of his Market Street stationers. And look at Lomax's amazing exhibition of cheeses and jams and lobsters and salmon, and wonder at the trouble everyone took to decorate their shops and the streets on such occasions as the Indian Fund Gala in 1900. Higginbottom's is a

Newtown Station. (Courtesy John Hemsworth)

picture, and as for Stafford's the ironmongers, well, is it any wonder that Mr Stafford won first prize for his efforts? The town is alive with 'God Bless Our Empire' banners, with bunting, union jacks and portraits of the Queen. And across the foot of Market Street, hanging between Alsop and Clayton's the decorators, and the Railway Inn, here is a popular legend fluttering in the breeze:

TODAY YOU ARE ASKED TO HELP THOSE WHO CANNOT HELP THEMSELVES. BRITISHERS ARE AT ALL TIMES READY TO ASSIST IN DESERVING CASES.

Photographs, freezing an instant and turning it into eternity. If, one hundred years ago when the shutter clicked, you were 7 or 17 or 70 years old, you would be so in perpetuity. If, when the camera blinked, you had not combed your hair, then you would forever be unkempt. If you were Marjorie Mason, Queen of Cotton, you would be

Helping those who cannot help themselves. New Mills supports the Indian Famine Fund in 1900. (Courtesy NMLHS)

Lomax's shopfront.

more than queen for a day, you would be eternally so; and if you were Bill Grace, dapper in your grey top-coat and white trilby, you would be dapper till the end of time. You – principal stove-pipe player in the Pickerwood Comedy Band – you will know how it feels to be blacked-up for ever and ever;

A Whit walk at the beginning of the 20th century packs Market Street. (Courtesy Bill Barton)

Eaton's, Boot and Shoemakers of High Street. Ladies' boots soled and heeled from 1s 8d, gents from 2s 9d. (Courtesy NMLHS)

and you – whoever you are – gloomily packing cotton at the Bate Mill Bleachworks – you will never smile again. You graceful ladies, standing on the market ground where the buses now wait, you will remain precisely there forever; and you, Joe Gizzie Bennett, will squat behind your little dancing drum till doomsday. Only moving pictures would have enabled us to discover what happened next, and although even at the dawn of the century, moving pictures were, appropriately, finding their way to New Mills, they would not be pictures of you.

In the domain of work, home and leisure, the

The Pickerwood Temperance Prize Band. Blacked-up for ever and ever... (Courtesy NMLHS)

Edwardian decade represented a lively period for New Mills. At work (though fortunes would ever be changeable) many of the older textile mills had once again adapted to a modern age with its contemporary materials, products and processes, while new companies had been created to provide for a shifting and expanding stream of consumers from engineers to chemists, to advertisers and decorators. Transport and communication industries accounted for much of the action, the calico printworks along the Sett and Goyt valleys employed hundreds of people, and some companies, Scattergood's for example – 'joiners, builders, contractors, monumental masons and dealers in building materials' – clearly believed that diversity held the key to commercial success. Up to the minute houses, complete with all mod cons, continued to be built, especially in the Newtown area, and the old Victorian cottages, a simmering hybrid of the dissolute and the decent, still clung to the flanks of the Torrs.

...and you – whoever you are – gloomily packing cotton at the Bate Mill Bleachworks – you will never smile again. (Courtesy NMLHS)

–oOo–

At the same time leisure activities flourished with many companies, churches and chapels providing a wide range of sports and hobby opportunities for employees or members. Five-a-side football clubs such as the Pingot Stingers, or the New Mills Flat Ribs, were heavily subscribed and fanatically supported. Thornsett United embarked upon an outstandingly successful chapter in its history, and New Mills Football Club, the Millers (originally New Mills St George's), was founded at the turn of the century. Expectations among supporters were high, and it was not unknown for the Millers to attract crowds of 3,000, or indeed for players to be seriously admonished by the extremely vociferous and dangerous-looking, umbrella-wielding ladies of Torr Top. Bowls tournaments, billiards competitions and cricket matches were all popular, and let it not be believed that the ladies of the district were exempt. Those with cricketing talent, for instance, were by no means restricted to teapot tipping and jam spreading. Oh no! They played – and played

hard. The likes of Miss Hawthorne, Miss Greenwood, Miss Felton and Miss Willis of the New Mills Lady Cricketers caused, one has heard, many a gentleman batsman from Ollersett to blanch.

For the musical members of the community, orchestras, chamber groups, choral societies and glee clubs were founded, while for the actresses and actors of the area a number of drama groups took to the boards. Meanwhile, for the cultured and studious, existing library facilities had proved inadequate, and thanks to a donation of £2,000 from Andrew Carnegie, the new library in Hall Street was accordingly opened in 1910.

Rock Street, Torr Top. (Courtesy John Hemsworth)

Images

A gathering of Primitive Methodists at the top of Dye House Lane. The White Hart Inn is on the left. (Courtesy Bill Barton)

A carnival procession at the top of Dye House Lane. (Courtesy David Williamson)

Your Rolls awaits! (Courtesy David Williamson)

A family portrait, 1910. Mr and Mrs Arthur Ashworth with sons Arnold and Cecil. (Courtesy New Mills Library)

Scattergood and Warringtons cart, carnival bound. A photograph taken by Mr Hirst of Birch Vale post office... 'special attention given to children, enlargements and portraits in oil and watercolours... the favour of your recommendation will be esteemed.'
(Courtesy David Williamson)

Strines Station, early in the 20th century. (Courtesy NMLHS)

Thomas Moor of New Mills. An enigmatic scene from Mrs Livesley's photographic collection. (Courtesy John Hemsworth)

St. George's Parish Church,
NEW MILLS.

THE

ANNUAL SERMONS

ON BEHALF OF THE

National Day and Sunday Schools,

WILL BE PREACHED

→ On Sunday, August 11th, 1901. ←

MATINS AND HOLY COMMUNION, 10-30; PREACHER:

REV. J. LIONEL KNOWLES, M.A.,
VICAR.

FIRST EVENSONG, 3 P.M.; PREACHER:

REV. S. W. WALTERS, B.A.,
CURATE IN CHARGE OF FERNILEE.

SECOND EVENSONG, 6-30 P.M.; PREACHER:

REV. E. C. COLLIER, M.A.,
VICAR OF DINTING.

Your attendance and kind support on behalf of the afore-
named Schools are earnestly solicited.

J. LIONEL KNOWLES, VICAR.
E. ARNFIELD, ⎫
H. BARBER, ⎭ CHURCHWARDENS.

(Courtesy New Mills Library)

One year later something even more wonderful happened, something quite extraordinary. Moving pictures finally came to town. Flickering, jumpy, silent. Larger than life. Nothing more than twitching shadows on a white screen, they could grip you with fear, convulse you with laughter, and drench you in tears. You would most likely weep for *The Girl Who Went Astray*, marvel at *The Cleaning of Scroggins House*, recoil at the terrible consequences to be endured *When Women Hate*, and tremble *In the Jaws of Death*. And as you perched on the very edge of your sixpenny seat, your sensations would no doubt be greatly magnified by Mrs Wilkes at her trusty piano, deftly, uncannily accentuating every mood, thought, action. How did she do it?

Two cinemas opened in New Mills in 1911: David Taylor's Empire and Hippodrome – which subsequently became the Art Theatre – in Jodrell Street, and the Picturedrome, adjacent to the Crown Hotel (entry through the market hall and up the stairs at the rear), managed by Mr Stratton Wells. A third cinema, on Union Road, would open in the early twenties and would eventually specialise in 'talkies'. But for the time being the silent screen prevailed. Programmes changed three times a week, seat prices ranged from 6d to 1s 3d, and both venues – each mindful of the other perhaps – strove to provide tip-top entertainment and, naturally, excellent value for money. In addition to the very latest 'feature' films, for example, you could watch history unfold via slide shows or newsreels – the sinking of the *Titanic* or the Coronation procession of George V (and how they cheered for their King). You might well be treated to a brass band presentation – possibly the New Mills Prize Band for the 'first house', the Thornsett Band for the second – or perhaps you could join in a sing-song led by the likes of Little Ivy Frances, or even – and this would be quite remarkable – the spectacle of 'two young ladies knitting, eating bananas or blowing a post horn while submerged in a tank of water'. On other occasions entire evenings would be given over to variety shows, musical comedies, and, from time to time, boxing or wrestling matches. In other words, you might be offered any entertainment, which was not – and this was the only stipulation – 'obscene, vulgar or immodest'. New Mills, it seemed, was set fair for the future.

Bizarre!

A Japanese Floral Bazaar was held in the schoolroom of the Mellor Road Providence Congregational Church in February, 1909.

At the time, the Reverend W.D. Edmonson (conscientious, candid, capable) had served as pastor for over 14 years, and his colleagues had included Mr Scorer (hopeful,

(All items courtesy New Mills Library)

high-principled, honourable), Mr Goodwin (frank, faithful, forbearing), Mr Walker (earnest, energetic, estimable), Mr Pollit (precise, practical, praiseworthy), Mr Hadfield (sincere, sociable, staunch), and the late Mr Stafford (revered, respected, remembered).

Five hundred copies of a souvenir handbook were printed to mark the occasion. Beginning with a proclamation – 'Coming into the Bazaar without paying is forbidden, but paying without coming in may be permitted' – the handbook is a fine example of Edwardian whimsy.

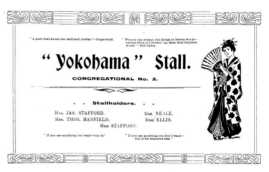

Home Sweet Home

Kinder View.

Ladyshaw House. (Courtesy Lorrie Marchington)

Watford Lodge and, above, Watford House. (Courtesy John Hemsworth)

Aspenshaw Cottages, Doctor's End, Thornsett. (Courtesy John Hemsworth)

Moscow Cottage. (Photo: Gwenda Culkin)

Looking over Bridge Street.

St Albans Street.

Doctor's End, Thornsett. (Courtesy John Hemsworth)

(Above, left and right) Goytside Farm.

Chapter 5
Theatre of the Absurd

THE names of many real people have appeared in these pages as the story of New Mills has unfolded. For, in spite of our having touched, albeit briefly, upon many facets of the area's development, it is as we have said, essentially the men and women of a place – those who celebrate its successes and share its troubles – who create and determine its character.

Here, then, are half a dozen more names to add to the plot.

William Jeffs, a porter at New Mills Central; a member of the St George's parish choir and of the Trades Hall Social Club.

Robert Buchanan, a sketch master at the Birch Vale Printworks and member of the High Peak Orpheus Glee choir.

Gilbert Pollard, rather scholarly; a pupil of New Mills Secondary School who, having passed the Oxford University entrance exam, decides instead to go to Manchester University. An enthusiastic athlete, who plays lacrosse for Disley, and cricket for New Mills, Gilbert is also an accomplished billiards player; and, it is said, a strong Liberal.

Joe Smith, who lives with his aunt and uncle on Spring Bank, and works at Birch Vale Printworks. Joe is a well-known footballer with Thornsett Juniors, and a tenor horn player with the New Mills Old Prize Band.

Robert Simister, a Co-operative Society architect, designer of the bakery at Newtown Co-operative. He too clearly enjoys his music and is a keen member of the Thornsett Primitive Methodist choir.

And George Clapham, an apprentice cabinet maker with Mr Sayer of Market Street; a good cricketer and a keen member of the Newtown Wesleyan chapel. Very well liked is George.

Six of the best! Strongly individual and different and yet, inevitably in such a close-knit community, also quite similar. Reading, drawing, designing, studying, engraving, labouring, shifting trunks, making furniture; working hard for a living; revelling in their football, cricket, billiards or lacrosse; supporting the Millers or the Colliers; attending evening classes, political meetings perhaps, and going to church or chapel on Sundays; singing in choirs or practising their instruments and playing in brass bands or string ensembles; possibly meeting friends at the social club; rummaging for bargains at the Saturday market; splashing out occasionally on an afternoon at the fair, on a train ride to Manchester or Buxton, or even on a day trip to Blackpool; probably dropping in at the Picturedrome, the Empire, or at the 'local' for a few drinks; almost certainly watching the girls go by. And finally – whatever their differences and similarities – being drawn together by circumstances beyond them and, along with 200 other young men of New Mills, getting themselves killed for king and country in World War One.

William Jeffs, in December 1917 after three months in France;

Robert Buchanan in Palestine in 1918;

Gilbert Pollard, 20, somewhere on the Somme in 1916;

Joe Smith, on his fourth stint at the front, having been wounded and sent home three times;

Robert Simister, in the last year of the war, on leaving his trench;

And George Clapham, 18 years old, in April 1917, after only one week in France.

They, and many hundreds beside, had come dashing down to the new recruitment centres. They had signed on at the police station, or at the Town Hall – anywhere they could – like eager young hopefuls desperate to shine at an audition. Many had put on their best suits and bowler hats, and as they queued, they laughed and joked as if they were guests at an engagement party. And in a sense they were, for signing on was a kind of betrothal to the cause.

Theirs was an overwhelming display of back-slapping, chest-swelling, hats-in-the-air, devil-take-the-hindmost patriotism, fired partly perhaps by certain images they may have seen at the local cinema, images depicting their nation's breathtaking military splendours. Nodding plumes and dazzling parades. Imperial pomp, and, inevitably, glory. They may have watched handsome regimental bands – the absolute personification of dignity – march across the screen, and looked on bedazzled as ranks of a thousand and more soldiers – the essence of invincibility – had presented arms in perfect unison; and they may have seen the great ships – Dreadnought perhaps – riding implacably over the heaviest seas, guns ablaze, and although they did not necessarily believe that war would have been quite like this, such images may have been the spur, and they would have shivered with goose pimples of pride. Add to this the great chorus of words – 'holy', 'honourable', 'right', 'just' – being trumpeted by the nation's leaders, the promise of travel, adventure and camaraderie, the burning expectations of their families and friends, and the certain knowledge that it would all be over by Christmas, and there is little wonder that to volunteer for action was regarded by many as a supreme privilege; little wonder that the concept of conscription was, for the time being at least, irrelevant.

And as the war advanced there would be men of substance and distinction to guide, inspire and protect them: Lloyd George, Churchill, French, Beatty, Allenby, Haig. Indeed, Lloyd George's mellifluous cadences had already begun to do the job. He had proclaimed this conflict to be nothing less than 'a crusade' – a fully costumed holy war to be waged on behalf of the 'little five foot five nations' of Europe. A holy war! How thrilling it must have seemed to have been awarded even the smallest walk-on part in this exalted drama.

Mr Arnfield, extreme right, owner of the Globe Engineering Works, together with his munitions workers. (Courtesy NMLHS)

So, the Woodwards and the Westalls, the Conways and Dysons, the Chattertons and Higginbottoms – aged 17 or 25, or even 50, leaving behind mothers and fathers, wives and children – forsake their cottages in Spout Gutter, Torr Top, Birch Vale and Brookbottom; and their farms at Laneside and Highfield and Piece; their mills and sidings and offices; perhaps to be shot or blown up, gassed or drowned; to die from heatstroke, pneumonia, gangrene or spinal meningitis; at Ypres, Alexandria, Madras, Salonika, Kut El Amara. Or perhaps even to survive yet be impaired forever.

Back at home the threat of Zeppelin attacks will, momentarily at least, subdue the townsfolk of New Mills; the gasworks steam whistle will stand by, ready to sound the alarm; and street lighting will be turned off in the interests of security. Women will be urged to join the workforce. Especially in munitions of course, but also in clerical tasks, administration and even engineering. When the war is over these things will be remembered and slowly and painfully – though it will need the inspiration of the Pankhursts or a Cavell – conditions for women in England will change forever.

In the local press families are urged: KEEP IN TOUCH WITH YOUR BOY IN THE TRENCHES BY SENDING HIM THE NEWS FROM HOME. SEND HIM THE *REPORTER*.

Charles Cooper's funeral procession. (Courtesy New Mills Library)

Charles Cooper

Charles Cooper, Private, 2595 1st/6th battalion Sherwood Foresters (Notts & Derby Regt). Died of Wounds, 1915. Aged 29. Son of Charles and Martha Cooper, of Torr Top. Husband of Elizabeth Cooper. Employed as an engraver at Messrs Walter Campbell's and Co. Works on St George's Road. Member of the New Mills Old Prize Band.

Charles Cooper was the first New Mills man to die in World War One.

(Stephen Lewis)

Charles Cooper of the Sherwood Foresters. (Courtesy George Cooper)

Meanwhile, the same families appear to accept news of dreadful casualties with impressive fortitude. This is partly due, no doubt, to the government's skilful use of propaganda, partly to a lingering popular belief in the integrity of the war and – perhaps most tellingly – to the courage and resilience shown by the fighting men themselves.

Letters from the trenches speak, inevitably, of the appalling conditions. The lakes of mud. The gas. The torrents of water. Of the nearness of death. The limbs of friends blown away in violent explosions. And yet they often do so in strangely matter of fact and understated ways – in a tone of resigned optimism.

'We are all looking forward to Christmas,' writes Alf Shaw in 1916, '...I am in the best of health, and feel fit enough for anything. But I won't be sorry when the war is over and I can return to dear old England'. Also in 1916 Jack Lawton anticipates 'better days in store... Never mind about us,' he says, 'we are alright. If we have to go under, we shall go. We are as happy as the next'.

Surely such front line composure must have made it hard, not to say impossible, for those at home to surrender to their own misfortunes, for to have done so would have demonstrated a personal frailty unworthy of the occasion.

But the world of 1914–18, both in the theatres of war, and on the streets of New Mills, is one of bizarre paradoxes.

While on Monday the union jacks of Bate Mill or Birch Vale Printworks might fly high above the rooftops – a noble gesture of defiance – on Tuesday they are lifeless and half-lowered in honour of Richard Barton or Walter Bates, former employees. On Wednesday, the New Mills Old Prize Band (now, proudly, a battalion band) might step out smartly – down Market Street and on to Union Road – their rousing renditions of patriotic songs provoking bursts of applause and perhaps even a little singing from passers-by; yet on Thursday the band, muted and muffled, leads the cortège of Norman Jones in a slow, slow march to St George's churchyard. Heads bowed, beside his grave they play *Nearer my God to thee*. Yesterday you may have joined in a high-spirited fancy dress procession in support of the war effort, yet today you are dressed in your weeds of mourning. Those fine voices which only moments ago swelled the choirs of St Mary's or St Luke's, now softly sing *Safe Home in Port* at the burial of Charles Leverington, stoker first class, Royal Navy. On Friday your factory turns out its paper cylinders or tin plate, while on Saturday it begins an emergency conversion for the production of bombs and shells. What is your splendid house today, may become, tomorrow, a makeshift hospital to receive the wounded. And on Sunday you will obediently gather to thank God.

These curious counterpoints – the normal and the freakish, the comic and the tragic – appear unremittingly in the newspapers of the day, and are so commonplace as to almost escape attention. In the *High Peak Reporter* of 21 July 1917, for example, the distressing story of a family whose first son is lost in action and whose second is 'permanently maimed' is set beside a lively account of the town's dazzling three-day carnival in aid of the Red Cross Hospital – an event for which literally thousands of people turn out to share in the fun and games. In view of its context, this great occasion deserves a little more of our attention.

On the Thursday and Friday of carnival week two so-called 'geranium days' raise over £100 for this 'most noble of causes', while on Saturday everyone's attention turns to the procession and gala. The procession, the biggest ever seen in New Mills, takes place in glorious summer weather. The Sunday schools, of which it is largely composed, have, it is said, 'vied with each other in producing the picturesque', and as the parade passes by, the spectators are enchanted by 'daintily adorned flower girls', Hindoos and Chinamen, and carefully-posed tableaux of military weddings; by shepherd boys and girls in red, white and blue; Irishmen, cowboys, Swiss misses and neat little Japanese girls; by Florence Nightingale and Father Time. And they are quite startled by the unexpected appearance of a full-sized South Seas island canoe!

They are amused by the wonderfully energetic nursery rhyme characters; charmed by the Rose Queen, Fairy Queen, Shamrock Queen, by Erin and Britannia; and elevated by the brightly embroidered banners – 'Lasting Peace' and 'God Grant Us Victory' – which are interleaved between the tableaux.

And finally, late in the procession, as the onlookers applaud Little Bo Peep and Tom Thumb, they will become aware of an approaching lurry which seems to be receiving even more attention than the others. As it comes closer a kind of euphoria appears to accompany it. People are cheering wildly and seem to be pressing to touch it as it passes… and now, at last, you too can see what it is carrying: wounded soldiers! Actual soldiers straight from battle. Pale and bandaged, waving to the crowds. Attended by their nurses. An exhibition of heroes received fervently by the public and acclaimed by the *Reporter* for bringing 'a touch of reality' to the great occasion.

Is this another scene from our theatre of affections or is it the theatre of the absurd?

The procession passes by and on the field next to the Town Hall the gala begins. There are concert parties, bands, singers, all manner of fairground rides, Aunt Sally rings, cups of tea and cream cakes.

Huge, fulsome crowds are milling around and making merry. Yet, as the *Reporter* points out, 'young men (are) conspicuous by their absence. And for a very good reason. They are away fighting for home and country'.

Now, if you had happened to live in New Mills in 1917, and if you had not, for one reason or another, experienced front line action, how would you have responded to all of this? What part would you have played in this strange, ambivalent regime? And when the war was over, and the victory parades were done, and when the emotional consensus which had driven it on had finally shattered, how would you have adjusted to the loss of two hundred of your youngest and strongest kinsmen, and to the everlasting incapacity of hundreds more?

Tor Top Tunnels

As the families of Torr Top struggled through World War One, many of its young men were abroad, demonstrating exceptional courage: sometimes such courage as would win high honours. John McQuaid and John Hibbert would gain the Military Medal, Edward Brown and Corporal John Cooper the Distinguished Conduct Medal. For such distinction 'Torr Top should be enshrined in the hearts of New Mills people,' declared the *High Peak Reporter* in 1919.

And indeed, so it would be. In October 2002 – 84 years after the Armistice – a memorial, commissioned by New Mills Town Council, would finally commemorate the brave men of Torr Top, and in a brief but moving ceremony, a simple, circular stone plaque would be unveiled by George Cooper, son of John Cooper.

Corporal Cooper, however, had another claim to fame. For it was he who, in a sense, had drawn Torr Top itself into the very heart of the battle – to Sanctuary Wood, near Ypres. War historian Stephen Lewis (who was largely responsible for bringing the memorial project to fruition) tells, in his much-respected *Debt of Honour*, how Cooper named his trench after the street in New Mills where he lived; how the words TOR TOP TUNNELS (sic)

Corporal John Cooper. (All items courtesy George Cooper)

In camp.

John Cooper, standing second from left, with his platoon.

A greeting to John.

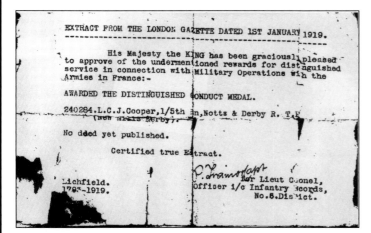

EXTRACT FROM THE LONDON GAZETTE DATED 1ST JANUARY 1919.

His Majesty the KING has been graciously pleased
to approve of the undermentioned rewards for distinguished
service in connection with Military Operations with the
Armies in France:-

AWARDED THE DISTINGUISHED CONDUCT MEDAL.

240284.L.C.J.Cooper, 1/5th Bn,Notts & Derby R. T.F.

No deed yet published.

Certified true Extract.

Lichfield.
1795-1919.

For Lieut Colonel,
Officer i/c Infantry Records,
No.6.District.

Notification of the award of Distinguished Conduct medal to 240284 L.C.J. Cooper.

were printed on a plain board, and were displayed – proudly, for all to see – at Hill 62; and how the name even appeared on a contemporary military map, becoming, in the process, a small part of wartime mythology. Tor Top Tunnels. A true home from home!

An official World War One military map showing Tor Top Tunnels.

*British Gallantry Awards
45th and 95th Foot
The Sherwood Foresters
Compiled by C. Housley Miliquest
Cooper, J. Lance Corporal 240284:
1/5th Battalion: London Gazette
1.1.1919: For conspicuous devotion to duty and consistent good work since September 16, to date. He had on several occasions as section commander showed very great gallantry in action and excellent leadership.*

Bravo Tor Top! (Photo © Gary Wood 2003)

The Royal British Legion

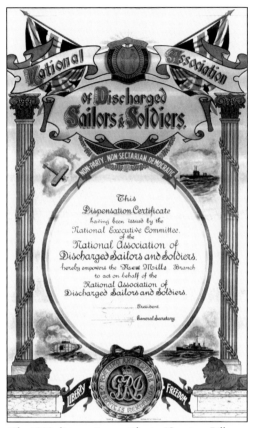

The 1918 dispensation certificate. (Courtesy Bill Robertson)

Bill Robertson on parade. (Courtesy Bill Robertson)

A founder member of the National Association of Discharged Soldiers and Sailors, New Mills was presented with a dispensation certificate by Arthur Jackson, the association's president, in 1918.

Three years later – again as a founder member – the New Mills branch became part of the British Legion, an organisation which gained a royal charter in 1971.

Gradually, and perhaps inevitably, the Legion's activities dwindled, until, in the late 1980s, two ex-servicemen – Jack Reeves (of the Royal Engineers), and Bill Robertson (of the Royal Tank Regiment) resolved to revive its fortunes.

Since Jack's death in 1995, Bill, a true and dedicated legionnaire, has continued to organise the branch's programme of events. There is now an active membership of 50, and meetings are held every quarter, though it must be said that activities are declining and Bill is not too optimistic about the Legion's future.

Chapter 6
Aftermath

Torr Top.

November 1918 – Peacetime

AND whom, do you think, was one of the first heroes of the peace? Why, Mr Taylor of the New Mills Empire, of course!

Indeed, almost before the ink of the Armistice was dry, Mr Taylor gathered together the 'kiddies of the town' and marched them, in a pied-piperly way, round the streets, flags and banners flying, straight into his theatre. Suddenly, after the dark days of wartime, the Empire was stuffed to the rafters with 'jubilant and grateful children' relishing the 'free patriotic concert' Mr Taylor had so generously provided for them. Accompanied by

Miss Elsie Taylor on the pianoforte, they sang all the airs of the day 'with rare gusto' and cheered 'the great spectacle of all the men (and women) of the Allies', reserving a 'tremendous shout for the late Lord Kitchener'. In contrast, the film *Four Years in Germany* gave the 'the kiddies their chance of showing their hostility towards German despotism, which they did in no uncertain manner'.

Mr Taylor made a brief reference to the glorious news that victory had crowned the Allies' efforts, and, although he knew that a host of patrons' hearts were sad through the loss of loved ones, he trusted that they would find some consolation in the fact that the supreme sacrifice of those they loved had not been in vain. He trusted that all present would... fervently sing the National Anthem'. After this the orchestra 'by a happy inspiration struck up *Rule Britannia.*'

Mr Taylor was heartily applauded for these remarks, and he concluded with the hope that everyone would rally round to support the two concerts he proposed to present on 5 January 'for the benefit of the War Shrine, to be erected... to perpetuate the memory of the heroes who had fallen in the great conflict'.

As for the week's cinematic attractions, *Durance of the Badlands* featuring Dustin Farnum, would 'grip the heart from start to finish', while *Monica's Past* – 'a charming story of love, pity and human pitfalls' – would be accompanied by the usual topical and comical films. At the end of the week, Pearl White's *The Fatal Ring* and *Four Years in Germany* instalment five, would maintain the high standards of entertainment people had come to expect from a visit to the Empire.

Hot off the mark was the flamboyant and popular Mr Taylor, but certainly no hotter than then the Church of England!

YOUR THANK OFFERING, HAVE YOU MADE IT?

What is to be your thank offering for victory?

You will, please God, for the sake of England's Immortal Dead,

lead a life of service to God and to your fellow men.

As a pledge of what you mean to do, you will join in contributing to your Church of England Fund of Five Million Pounds by which the businessmen of the Church mean to make the Church of England strong in her work of reconstruction.

Cheques were to be made out to the Church of England Central Fund, and addressed to Canon Partridge at Sanctuary House.

During those last few weeks of 1918, people must have felt very confused as regards their startling change of fortune. Despite the fanfares and celebrations they may have discovered that their earlier notions of peace had not quite been in accord with its sudden reality. They may have wondered why their new condition was less... less... less what? – why their condition was less

reassuring than they had anticipated it would be. Why had the victory not been able to dissipate that feeling of apprehension they had carried around with them for the last 52 months? Perhaps, as the balloons began to wrinkle and the banners fray, their sense of purpose had finally begun to waver, their determination to weaken, and maybe at last they began to realise they were weary with a weariness that sleep could not cure.

Perhaps they had even begun to ask what it had all been for, and what would happen now. After all, a number of young men were still abroad and, although the war was over, for many families it was not safely so, since the likes of the Staffords, the Pikes and the Peels had yet to receive the crushing news about Joseph, Ernie and Robert.

On the streets, as the shortening days delivered a kind of backwash to victory people may have become more and more aware of an emotional uncertainty among their fellows. Their quest for normality must have been an eerie, self delusory one, for they must surely have known – even as they dressed for their Christmas socials – that in every street there were doors behind which untold suffering was secreted. Laughter must have been hollow, conversations guarded, for even if – a slender chance – they had not lost someone dear or at least known to them, the person beside them may not have been so fortunate, and the girl across the table may have been grieving for someone quite irreplaceable.

And if you had been in the situation of having lost a son or a husband, would you not now have begun to feel disconnected by your fate and, despite yourself, to have thought, if only occasionally, 'There's Alice Walker's boy... it's alright for some people'?

The Providence Memorial Window

The World War One memorial window in the Mellor Road Providence United Reform Church.

TO THE GLORY OF GOD AND IN HONOURED MEMORY OF THE MEN OF THIS CHURCH WHO GAVE THEIR LIVES IN THE GREAT WAR 1914 – 1919.

Ernest Brocklehurst, Joseph Smith, Frank Conway, Joseph Stafford, Harry Conway, Wilfred Walker, Squire Buckley Liddiard, William Woodward, William Liddiard, John Henry Woodward ALSO IN GRATEFUL RECOGNITION OF THE OTHERS WHO SERVED AND WHOSE LIVES WERE MERCIFULLY SPARED

The Providence Memorial window. (Photo: Barbara Matthews)

–oOo–

Though it is not possible to detect much of this in the actual events of the time, there is a sense in which those events appear as fragments, which do not quite knit together.

There is a strike at Brunswick Mill, and a collection in aid of the strikers is said to have raised a 'good sum'.

Little Mary Plant, aged four, is run over by a motor vehicle(!), the Co-operative Society's van driven by the hapless Mr Wharmby.

A memorial service, conducted by the Reverend Lionel Knowles, is held at the Market Ground, to give thanks for the 'cessation of hostilities'.

Several deaths from influenza are reported.

Newtown School proudly announces a lecture recital to be given by Casey, the world-renowned violinist and speaker. It will be called 'The Mission of the Minstrel'.

At a governors' meeting held at New Mills Secondary School, teachers' salaries are discussed. It is suggested that a starting salary of £160, rising to a ceiling of £600 via increments of £15, is a fair and equitable arrangement.

Prisoners of war begin arriving home, many with shocking stories of their treatment.

Handel's *Messiah* is performed at the Town Hall.

There is not a single bottle of Bovril left in New Mills.

Memorial services are held at many churches.

MARY PICKFORD VISITS NEW MILLS roar the posters, sadly, only on film, however, in her greatest creation, 'Stella Maris'.

Old folks parties are reinstated.

Amy Burgess, pupil of Florence Wyatt LLCM, is successful in gaining honours for the intermediate exam of practical music.

Torr Vale Mill temporarily closes for lack of yarn. This is due to cotton strikes elsewhere.

DON'T LOOK OLD an advertiser pleads. LOCKYER HAIR RESTORER darkens to the former colour in a few days.

There are photographs in the newspaper of soldiers who have been reported dead since the Armistice.

A 'simply brilliant' Hallé concert takes place at

Ollersett View in 2003 after its conversion into 'desirable apartments'.

the Town Hall. Encores, however, are not permitted on account of the train times.

Casey is so famous that he has even performed in Iceland! His visit will be a real treat for music lovers.

Employees at the Print and Bleachworks are to be given a most generous holiday, from Christmas Eve to 6 January.

A Victory Ball held at the Town Hall on Christmas Eve attracts 'large numbers of devotees of the light fantastic toe'!

At a meeting of the Food Committee milk sellers are warned not to increase their prices, while the Division Committee indicates that an extra ton of jam and marmalade has been allocated to New Mills.

Ollersett View Hospital (the former Low Leighton workhouse) before refurbishment.

The Golf House. (Courtesy New Mills Library)

New Mills Golf Club

New Mills Golf Club, Shaw Marsh. A thousand feet up. Kinder to the east. The Welsh hills to the south west. As dramatic as could be.

It was 1906 when Charlie Hudson applied for a license to rent parts of Sam Hancock's farmland 'for the purpose of playing golf.' The application went through without a hitch, but with certain provisos: namely that farmer Hancock be allowed to keep as many horses, cattle and sheep on the land as he thought fit; that the licensee be liable to pay compensation for any such animal hit by golf balls; and that Mr Hancock be admitted to full membership of the proposed golf club, being 'entitled to all benefits without paying any entrance fee or

Ladies' Day. (Courtesy New Mills Golf Club)

The Golf House from Eaves Knoll Road. (Photo © Gary C. Wood, 2003)

subscription.' Not that this would be a one-sided contract. On the contrary, in return, farmer Hancock would undertake to refrain from ploughing up the land in question, to make available a small clubroom above the farm's wash-house, to make teas for members (except on Sundays), and to abide by the club's rules of conduct.

An additional clause in the 1906 license would permit members to extend the proposed nine-hole course to 18 holes (when they 'thought it proper to do so'). Accordingly, land would be reserved for this purpose. And indeed, an 18-hole course (though not on the original land) was duly opened... on 9 June 2002, 96 years later!

In the meantime there had been many changes. As early as 1909 the first clubroom had been re-sited – in one of the two cottages on the corner of Apple Tree Road in which it still resides; running water had been laid on in 1938; in 1949 the club had finally purchased the land upon which it stood; and in 1952 electric lighting had replaced the old paraffin lamps.

A diverting account of the club's history is to be found in *Caddie to Captain to Veteran* (1996) in which Harold Froggatt records an association dating back nearly 70 years. He recalls the hardships of the old times, the best of the players – both gents and ladies; club characters and benefactors; and how he himself rose from caddie in the 1930s, to captain in 1961.

Once upon a windy afternoon. Sheila Atkinson and Mary Cooper. (Courtesy New Mills Golf Club)

Harold, now a veteran, has arranged – when the appointment comes – to have his ashes scattered on the course, and warns future players to beware where they tread. But for now he continues to play at the club – which is as friendly and unpretentious as one can imagine – looking forward, no doubt, to sampling the hospitality of the new club house planned for the near future.

A constellation of captains. The opening of the new course in 2002. (Courtesy New Mills Golf Club)

An old lady turns up at a polling centre to vote. She would like to vote for Lloyd George. The presiding officer shows her a ballot paper and tells her she must vote for either Major Hill Wood or Captain Brooks. 'But I want to vote for Lloyd George,' she says.

Jas Higginbottom pleads for the establishment of a Role of Honour Fund.

Football clubs are re-established and golfers are back on the hills.

The Creation is performed at the New Mills Primitives.

Bands and carol singers crowd the streets, the Christmas mails are heavy, and there are parties at Sunday schools. Soldiers at the Red Cross Hospital are treated royally, as are the inmates at Ollersett View. Many soldiers who have remained in France and Belgium come home for Christmas to heroes' welcomes and 'those who have passed hence' are not forgotten. 'Wreaths and evergreens are laid at the War Shrine near the parish church gates, creating a beautiful and pathetic expression of Christmas memories.'

Mr Taylor presents a very special coup at the Empire. 'The most historic event in the annals of our island history will be revealed in an exclusive film showing the surrender, to Admiral Sir David Beatty, of the German High Seas Fleet. Only a few were privileged to witness this historic event, but it has been carefully photographed for the millions to gaze upon, and New Mills has its great opportunity this coming week'.

Casey, the world-renowned violinist, sadly does not turn up for his famous lecture recital, 'The Mission of the Minstrel', at Newtown School. 'He will, however, visit New Mills next Friday and all those who get a chance to hear him are assured of a rich treat'.

–oOo–

Cyril Bowden was born on 12 December 1915 and baptised three weeks later at St George's Church on 5 January 1916. His parents, Frank and Margaret Bowden of Low Leighton, were probably – though one can only suppose – absolutely delighted by the new arrival. Yet wartime was not the best of times for family celebrations and Frank, having already seen active service in the Boer War, was called upon once again, on this occasion to join the conflict in Europe. The gods being firmly hitched to his side, however, he survived this second assignment and duly returned home in 1918 to re-engage with his family and friends, to revive his somewhat fitful career in copper rolling and polishing, and to pursue those so-often-longed-for everyday routines of peacetime, routines ordinary and mundane perhaps, but at least without serious hazard.

As far as the war itself was concerned, thankfully one could at last put it aside in the knowledge that ultimately justice had been done, lessons had been learnt, and apparently, rational resolutions adopted. The League of Nations, an international court of law, would identify and dismantle any future threats to peace and so, in a sense, the 'war to end all wars' would finally have justified its promise.

Little did Mr and Mrs Bowden know, however, that in reality neither good intentions, nor treaties, nor international assemblies could control the extremes of human ambition, and that soon after their son had come of age, the whole ghastly business would be ready to begin again.

By 1939 Cyril Bowden was married – to a young woman called Edith Allen – and had found employment as a pentagrapher at Campbell's

Engraving Company. But, as World War Two gathered pace, he found himself, just as his father before him, drawn into the turmoil of a European battlefield.

–oOo–

It is certainly true to say that during the inter-war years – a period which encompassed practically the whole of Cyril Bowden's life – there were happy times, times of laughter, humour and good fortune. But equally it cannot be denied that, on the whole, both locally and nationally, this was a gloomy, anxious age, one of changing priorities and values, of looking forward, standing still and backtracking all at once.

Dazzling innovations – ELECTRIC LIGHTING, MOTOR VEHICLES, GRAMOPHONES, FLUSH TOILETS – claimed the headlines, but even as they did so they were accompanied and often grimly abrogated by an unpleasant and persistent opposition – DEBT, POVERTY, STRIKES, DEPRESSION, ECONOMIC COLLAPSE.

True, New Mills had emerged from World War One a cut above the rest of the industrial communities of the High Peak, but she could hardly be expected to withstand for any length of time the downward pressures of what was after all a national crisis, and soon she was haunted by the realities of unemployment and privation, and in due course, by the demise of such large-scale employers as Wirksmoor Mill, Watford Bridge Printworks and Brunswick Mill, not to mention a whole clutch of smaller companies.

How much of this, one wonders, was apparent in the daily life of the ordinary New Mills inhabitant? Cyril Bowden, for example. What kind of place did he grow up and live in? What would have concerned and amused his parents and friends? What issues would have defined the inter-war years for these people? When in 1922 Cyril Bowden was seven, for instance (and no doubt totally oblivious to history!) what was actually going on round about as he went off to school or played street football with his brothers?

Brookside – a photo sketchbook

(All photos courtesy John Hemsworth)

Chapter 7
1922

Hyde Bank Mill.

IN 1922 you cannot fail to be aware that in the very midst of deprivation and economic gloom, a new world is beginning to rise from the debris of the old. In magazines and newspapers, at the cinema, in shops and showrooms – although many of the people around you will be unable to provide shoes for their feet and meat for their table – you will be besieged and seduced by new notions, enterprises and opportunities; fashions, fabulous machines and amazing inventions.

If you are a woman you will find – in the *High Peak Reporter* for example – a vast army of ideas and articles devised especially for you. Lady Alison's Fashion Boudoir will surprise and uplift you, while Miss Marjorie Maynard's exclusive designs – 'a very useful frock in lemon', 'a particularly charming gown' – will take your breath away. You will be taught how best to treat your chipped nails or your chapped hands, how to smell sweet, to stay fresh and how to protect your complexion.

If you are a man you will be bewitched by voluptuous illustrations of motor cars, spotless and gleaming, heady with intent: the Touring GN for £225, the All Weather model, the Dual Purpose GN and, at £240, the Leger Sports car. Feast your eyes upon its contours. Think of it. Drive it. Speed. Luxury. The freedom of an open road. A secret journey to share with your chosen companion. 'It is sweet to be alive these days'. And intoxicating. Yet, for most of you it is also meaningless! All you can do is stare, covet and make fantasies.

If, however, you do actually own a motor car – and some people do – you may soon discover that an intoxicating fantasy is less robust than a sober truth. For, during this very spring a car, driven 'at considerable velocity' through our town, has turned a somersault in the street. The driver and his young lady passenger have been seriously hurt. In another incident a chauffeur has been charged with manslaughter following the death of a pedestrian. In a third, a car has collided with a lamp post bringing the lamp itself down onto the roof of the vehicle.

And, in addition to such misfortunes, it is reported that some of our less well-off neighbours – the disaffected ones – have learned to steal components from parked cars and lorries, and to dispose of them via secret traders who wait in the shadows.

Motor car or not, the freedom of the countryside can still be yours, for in 1922, much to the chagrin of the so-far-monopolistic railway companies, 'speedy motor coaches with pneumatic tyres are making travel by road truly enjoyable'. Birch Vale Printworks, among others,

hires these spanking new coaches for workers' trips to Blackpool, Matlock and Chester, and it is generally agreed that 'a chara ride in the country has never yielded more delight'. In the meantime – unsure of how to cope with competition so alarming – railway proprietors attempt to woo you back to the track with a feast of cheap and consciously cheeky deals.

In the sphere of amazing inventions, science is on the march. Science is chic! Man Zan, the wonder pile remedy, is popularly known as 'Science in a tube'; California Syrup of Figs, as 'Science in a bottle'. Most astonishing of all, however, we are told that soon Ultimate Science, world-changing science, will be upon us. In the

Happy Ever After?

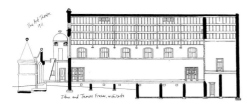

The architect's drawing of 1911. (Courtesy Town Hall)

How colourless life would have been without them! We would never have known the palaces of Siam, or the islands of the South Pacific. There would have been no breezy sailors or painted geishas. No little maids from school; no Jets, no Sharks.

Had it not been for them we would not have seen such carnivals and clambakes; would never have marched all day or danced all night; or have spied upon such tangled love affairs. Were it not for them the Sahara would have remained a mirage, and Brigadoon would never have stirred. And all those finely tuned cross-purposes, mistaken identities and happy-ever-after-endings would have passed us by.

Since their formation in 1922 they have brought us 75 dynamic seasons, 150 tremulous opening nights, and a thousand expectant overtures. They have won prizes for *Fiddler on*

The Art Theatre following the refurbishment of the 1980s. (Courtesy NMDODS)

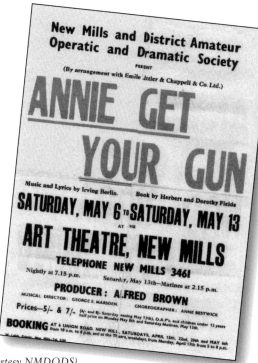

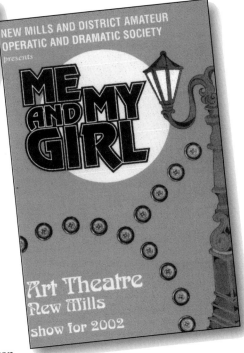

(Courtesy NMDODS)

the *Roof*, *Hello Dolly*, *My Fair Lady*, and have even
– with the help of their many Friends and Members – bought a theatre of their own and turned
it into a gem.

The history of the New Mills and District Operatic and Dramatic Society (thankfully usually known as the Amateurs!) is inextricably linked with the Art Theatre in Jodrell Street. Built in 1911, (as the New Mills Empire and Hippodrome), the theatre is not exactly a vision of beauty.

It stands rather glumly on a site besieged by terraced houses and huddled vehicles, a little out of sorts with its surroundings. Yet, herein may lie its secret – its very bleakness a dramatic device contrived to magnify its internal beauty. For step through the glass and your world will be transformed...

It was in the early 1980s that the Amateurs began to pour their resources into an intensive programme of theatre restoration and refurbishment. Since then improvement has followed improvement and has included not only the installation of sophisticated sound and lighting systems, but a much-envied revolving stage.

Yet a theatre, however fine, is bricks and mortar. It takes talent and energy to bring it to life. Fortunately, the Amateurs have an abundance of such things.

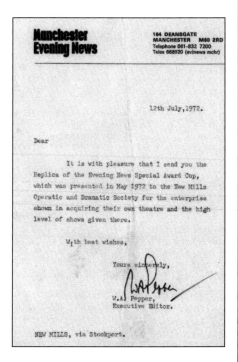

press it is announced, with a certain degree of gravitas that we should prepare for nothing less than a revolution:

> Within a few weeks it will be unnecessary to go to Manchester to hear a great singer or speaker. It will not even be necessary to move outside one's home. The voice of the singer or speaker will be brought into the home, though the singer or speaker are separated from us by a distance of several miles...

This exciting news carries fast, and in no time at all a wireless club is established which (New Mills being New Mills) becomes so buoyant that it cannot find a room large enough to accommodate its eager members.

Speaking of singers, it appears that in 1922 New Mills is a virtual paradise for the amateur musician and concert-goer. During this dismal year an operatic society is formed, 'jazz bazaars' with musical entertainment take place, and – of all the incredible things – the sale of pianos flourishes!

Imagine it. We are in the grip of an economic vice, bakers and butchers are falling by the wayside, factories are slamming their gates, yet Bates Piano Company can not only afford to decorate the shop, but Mr Bates can show you a nice rosewood upright for £48 10s 0d or even, perhaps, a magnificent 'Angelus' player piano, complete with 40 music rolls, for a mere £21 0s 0d!

Churches, Sunday schools and other organisations are, musically speaking, as active as ever, and, what with productions of *Merrie England* and *The Gondoliers*, performances of large orchestral works, and recitals of Schubert songs, with band concerts taking place in every nook and cranny, with centres for music festivals and examinations on the increase, little wonder the *Reporter* is moved to comment, 'no country town in England is so rich and fortunate in its musical organisations as New Mills'.

However, the churches, for once unified in protest, do draw the line at a proposed palais de danse. 'I'm no killjoy,' says vicar Lionel Knowles, and 'I have no objection to dancing under proper supervision...' But this! A dance hall! Consider its

The Millers

In the late 1880s the first organised football teams began to appear in New Mills, and by the end of the century, the Millers – already playing semi-professional football – were importing players from other clubs, much to the annoyance of some of the local lads who were paid less!

Later, such players as Harry Harding (New Mills, Stockport County, Everton and England), and even, perhaps, Walter Winterbottom – who, according to club secretary Allan Jones, may have begun his playing career with New Mills – attracted

(All items courtesy NMAFC)

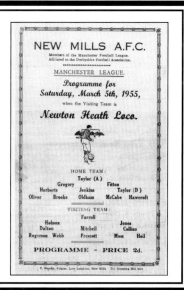

large crowds, at first to Mill Fields, and after 1921 to the Church Lane ground.

And New Mills FC have continued – especially during the Joe Martin years – to attract a level of support disproportionate to their status. The recent grant-aided installation of flood lighting and of an all-weather pitch has immeasurably improved the ground – of which, unusually, the Millers are proud owners – and may well have inspired them to another golden age.

Honours

Manchester League Premier Division Champions
1924 1926 1956 1963 1965 1966 1967 1968 1970 1971

Runners up
1925 1928 1953 1961 1962 1972 1974

Manchester League First Division Champions
1968 1972

Runners up
2001

Gilgryst Cup Winners
1960 1964 1965 1967

Shield Winners
1960 1965 2002

Open Trophy Winners
1972

Derbyshire Cup Winners
1921 1923 1924 1928 1948 1988 2001 2002

Derbyshire Junior Cup Winners
1997

Derbyshire Senior Cup Finalists
1940 1955 1967 1977

Manchester Amateur League Champions
1940

Manchester Amateur Cup Winners
1940 1949

Manchester Amateur League Cup Winners
1940

Manchester Junior Cup Winners
1952 1955 1960 1965 1971

North West Youth Alliance League Winners
2000 2002

North West Youth Alliance Division 1 Cup Winners
2002

The Millers championship team of 1926, winners of the Manchester League Trophy.

The Millers, 1974.

effect on the moral tone of the neighbourhood! Accordingly, the palais is abandoned – though to the obvious displeasure of many. 'The trouble with the church these days', observes a certain 'Castle Edge', is that 'there is too much THOU SHALT NOT and too little THOU MAYEST IF THOU CHOOSEST'. Castle Edge! We shall hear more of him in due course.

On the other hand a new cinema – made of fireproof steel and concrete, lit by electricity, seating 723 people, and said to be 'the last word in comfort' – opens on Union Road, with Mary Pickford and 'Little Lord Fauntleroy' luminescent in radiant Prizma colour. At the same time the Art Picture Playhouse (formerly Mr Taylor's Empire) rises above such unbridled razzamatazz and devotes an entire week to Shakespeare.

In addition to the many opportunities for cultural pursuits, sporting interests are also well served. Tennis and women's hockey are increasing in popularity, bowling and golf are played with real passion, while cricket, both on and off the field, is close to a religious experience. But football is the GREAT game. In a plethora of leagues, countless matches per season are supported by thousands of spectators. Football is a phenomenon.

And what if you happen to be a child, as indeed Cyril Bowden is, at this time? Will you be pushed aside and forgotten? Certainly not. There are music and drama and sports clubs in plenty, children's cinema programmes, concert parties, Sunday school outings, and even your own personal newspaper column. For it is in February 1922 that the ubiquitous Uncle Ben makes his entrance.

Hello boys and girls! Here is something new for you. Games, pictures, puzzles, competitions, prizes. Teddy and golly will have their little antics recorded and you will enjoy many a hearty laugh at their screamingly funny tricks.

Or, Cyril, if that is too infantile for you, please punctuate the following: that that is is that that is not is not that that is.

–oOo–

The education system, however, or at least the teachers within it, are not gaining universal approval at this particular moment. Typically, it is not the actual quality of their work that is an issue but their 'high' salaries, short hours and long holidays. 'Salaries must be cut', huffs one enraged detractor. In the case of overstaffing, teachers must be redeployed, and, although this might appear harsh, 'married lady teachers ought to be the first to suffer'.

Does anyone know or care that during this very term one teacher at Thornsett has 57 pupils in his charge, and that he 'can do justice neither to himself nor to his class'?

And does anyone know or care that some teachers are working for at least 60 hours a week, and that ever so many are doing wonderful and imaginative things? Mr Hinde, the headmaster of Newtown Primary School, for example, has brought 'child-centred' education to New Mills. Much inspired by scientific developments, he has set up in his school hall a veritable wonderland of pulleys, balances, sundials and gears to tempt his pupils to get involved with, to touch and feel science. 'At dusk,' reports one awed spectator, the room takes on 'a strange and magical look, the objects in it [appearing] like living things, sharing the personality of their maker'.

Which leads us, I suppose, to the sterner side of New Mills in 1922, where serious debates and events occur, and in some areas, darker conditions prevail.

Pertinent modern issues are at the forefront of discussion; pollution of the atmosphere from noxious emissions, the retention or abolition of 'summertime', and – particularly since this is a General Election year – matters like proportional representation, and the role of women both in and beyond politics. The thesis is current, for instance, that 'housework is an infallible cure for neurasthenia and hysterical women' and that 'scrubbing [is] good for the ailing mind'.

Naturally, many women are inclined to disagree with this!

In party politics the High Peak Liberals adopt Lady Barlow – wife of experienced MP Sir J.E. Barlow – as their prospective parliamentary candidate. Womanhood notwithstanding, she is received cordially, especially since she is, according to Mr Farrington (a Chinley Liberal), clearly 'the best man for the job'.

The election itself, incidentally, is a three-horse race: Lady Barlow, Sir Samuel Hill Wood (Conservative) of Moorfield – the sitting MP, and the only local candidate, and Frank Anderson (Labour) – a late entry – the first 'red' candidate ever to compete in the Peak.

The campaign is punctuated with references to women – 'our dear lady members,' the 'wonderful women of our party', the 'fairer sex' – and when finally Sir Samuel addresses a victory celebration in New Mills he is even moved to attribute the greatness of his majority to his beloved ladies.

It has been a good campaign, and a fair one, but it must be said that Lady Barlow has come third. One wonders, on hearing the whispered questions, could this be partly due to her gender?

–oOo–

We have occasionally referred to the privations of 1922 – austerity, poverty, economic exhaustion – and may have implied that these conditions did not only impinge upon but actually defined the character of the time. Is it not curious, then, that they have not substantially inhibited our story? And is it not even more curious that in spite of them (and they are not imagined) such a positive picture of New Mills has emerged? Yet it remains true that, after all is said and done, 1922 was a harsh and sorrowful year, a year whose underlying affection was melancholy.

'Why have we got into this dreadful state?' asked the *Reporter*. 'Instead of a promised land of peace and prosperity, nothing but strife, depression, unemployment... We have not got a land fit for heroes to live in, and there are millions of starving and workless people'.

–oOo–

In 1922 the steep hillsides of the river are crowded with dark, foul-smelling slums and someone asks, 'When will the people who live there' be allowed out 'into the light and fresh air?' Far from enjoying the comforts of flushing toilets and electricity, the inmates here share degrading and disgusting earth closets, and many do not have even a gas supply.

In 1922, starved of financial resources, the council can build only a handful of houses for the poor, and can barely begin to scratch the surface of the accommodation problem.

In 1922 so-called 'good news for the unemployed' amounts to a few ex-servicemen being given preference for employment, at a half-penny an hour, on the Hague Bar sewerage project.

In 1922 railway and printing workers are in dispute with management; teachers – their salaries slashed – are deserting their profession; rivers are polluted with effluent; the air is poisoned by foul gases; and people trail down Station Road begging for free coke from the gasworks.

In 1922 the mysterious High Peak commentator, Castle Edge, (whom we briefly met a little time ago), directs a scalding attack at 'back scratching' and 'self congratulatory' members of the New Mills Council. He may not be fair, he may not even be accurate, but he is persuasive.

'You had a dream,' he writes. 'No more were mill chimneys to belch forth black smoke on our main street. We were to have our mills driven by water-produced electricity, our houses and streets were to be lighted by it, our heating and cooking done by the same agency. New Mills was to be the first smokeless town in England', a town 'fit for heroes to live in'.

'We were to have parks, playing fields, a memorial to our glorious dead, tracts of land for the games of the young, comfortable benches where the old could sit, rest and reflect, and a workhouse which would be no more than a memory. Education was to thrive, not only as a means to earn a living, but to serve its recipients as a joy for life. All of this has gone west!'

'And how you have preached economy. Yet the rates you levy are the highest in the town's history.

'You have even compelled a poor ex-serviceman who somehow found the will and energy to open a chipped-potato range in Newtown, to close it down.

'There are important things needing attention, things of greater value to our community than… a chipped potato range in a cottage. Wake up! A great adventure awaits you. Recover your vision splendid and give us the beautiful New Mills of your dream.'

Councillors are desperate to discover the identity of their articulate and passionate adversary. Councillor Hallawell promises not only to refute every sentence, but also to 'make mincemeat' of Castle Edge should their paths ever cross.

–oOo–

1922 whimpers to a close, and although the *Reporter* strives for a few moments of optimism – trade is showing signs of revival; there is promise of more work; and taxation is not so heavy as it was – nevertheless, one particular paragraph seems best to encapsulate the spirit of the time:

> We shall not mourn the dead year. It will pass with but few regrets. There is still much suffering in our midst. We do not look upon a settled world, but one which bears all the signs of a terrible upheaval… and [above our town] clouds still hang thick and heavy.

Chapter 8
A Town in Waiting

1930...1938

TO CONTINUE:

It is 1930. Lionel Knowles opens the eagerly awaited parish hall.

Council members discuss the housing problem, with particular reference to slum clearance.

Goldilocks meets the three bears at the Art Theatre.

Both the Thornsett Carnival and the New Mills/Hayfield cricket match are spoilt by rain.

The film version of *The Desert Song*, in its original 'Vitaphone' glory, ravishes audiences at the Union Road Cinema.

The *Reporter* offers readers instructions on how to use the telephone, ('talk distinctly but not too loudly... enunciate consonants,' and remember it is also very important 'to teach your maid the correct way of answering a call').

In a blatant case of shebeening* the Council imposes a fine on the shebeener.

The umpteenth *Messiah* is performed by church groups, while the Operatic Society stages the *The Geisha*.

The town's electricity supply is at last, at long last, switched on – 'without ceremony'.

And finally, during an August heat wave councillors remove their jackets and conduct business 'in their shirt sleeves'.

But stop! What is this? A time warp? Can eight whole years really have passed since we last dipped into the rituals of our town? True, there is some evidence of change – Lionel Knowles is now the 'late' vicar of New Mills; *The Desert Song* is a talkie; yes, telephones are a novelty; and the vision of councillors in shirt sleeves is truly historic – but, by and large, does it not seen that time has been, so to speak, adjourned, and that New Mills has become a town 'in waiting'?

This impression – of a slightly uneasy status quo – would seem to be substantiated in a December edition of *Echoes of the Peak*.

'Except in the shop windows,' the writer

* Shebeening: selling illicit home-made alcohol

The Old Hague Bar Fire Station.

service commenced. First fire engine named *Susan*. Fire and ambulance station on Hague Bar Road opened.

1928: New Mills Town Council empowered to supply electricity to inhabitants.

1929: Closure of Hayfield Union Workhouse… which becomes a mental hospital.

Perhaps – although these hardly constitute landmarks – we could have added that during the period in question no fewer than 124 council houses had been built at High Hill and Bakehurst (not a bad record under the circumstances); that evening classes had enjoyed a revival in popularity; that the Workers' Educational Association had established a New Mills branch; and, on an entirely different tack – can you believe this? – that male voice choirs were on the increase!

begins, 'there is not much evidence of Christmas about.' The depression in trade is 'the skeleton in the cupboard,' and it is sad to report that printers, bleachers and dyers have all been forced to accept a 15% reduction in wages. But after such a war as we have known, 'things cannot be straightened out in a short time.' Perhaps soon 'we shall reach rock bottom,' and be able to discover a 'new basis', a 'new level' for our affairs.

Is it not for all the world as if we were still locked into 1922? As a matter of fact between the end of 1922 and the beginning of 1930, significant 'landmarks in the history of New Mills' are conspicuously scarce, and even the Town Council's own publication, *New Mills 1894–1994*, can manage only the following:

1927: New Mills Urban District Council fire

The New Mills steamroller, NU3041, served the community for 40 years before retirement in the mid-1960s. From time to time it may still be seen at rallies and carnivals. (Courtesy NMLHS)

According to Bill...

Bill Barton was born in Lea Street in 1924. When he was three months old the family moved – next door – where he has lived ever since. According to Bill, 'New Mills was a grand place to be as a child. We'd play football, relivo and rallio, go down the quarry, make bonfires. And we'd swim in the stream up at Golden Springs by Briar Grove.'

Bill Barton at the end of 2002.

'In the 30s – if you knew the driver – you could ride in the delivery wagons. I went with Redfern's to Newcastle-upon-Tyne, and even to London. And in 1938 brother Ernest got a second-hand car, a 1930 Austin 7 … VV54,' Bill added, proudly recalling the numberplate.

Bill in 1943. (All items courtesy Bill Barton)

After Board School, Bill was awarded a scholarship and 'tried the Grammar School… but it wasn't my line.' Nor was laboratory work at Birch Vale Printworks where he lasted only five weeks, before applying to become an apprentice baker at the Co-op. 'I didn't get the job, but they put me in furnishing – 12s 8d a week.' From the very first day his fate was sealed: 'I had to go down to the boiler, clean it out, riddle the cinders and chop the firewood. After a cup of tea I was shown the accumulator, and after lunch I helped load the delivery vans. Next thing, I was allowed to go out with the wagon. Then, back to the shop until 7pm.' Marvellous! Meanwhile Bill, normally a peace-loving lad, had been thrown out of Sunday School for fighting.

W. and J.M. Barton's shop at the beginning of the 21st century.

Harry Keeling and 'whistling' Dick Morelle off to the carnival, Thornsett, 1932(?).

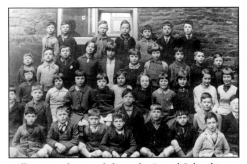

Bill Barton, bottom left, at the Board School in 1933.

At the outbreak of war he joined the LDV (Local Defence Volunteers, nicknamed 'Look, Duck and Vanish') which later became the Home Guard. 'Eventually we got 10 uniforms, 10 Canadian Ross rifles, and 10 tin hats, which after our turn of duty we had to leave at the Drill Hall for the next lot... First come, first served.' Bill was a runner and later a dispatch rider with the Home Guard, and when on duty at the Town Hall, he was the only one allowed out. 'I'd go for the chips and beer,' he said.

In 1943 Bill joined the Merchant Navy and travelled round the world. But, to be honest, getting home was always top of his agenda, and after the war he returned to furnishing, becoming, in succession, branch manager at Chapel-en-le-Frith Co-op, (where he met his future wife, Jean) and then furnishing manager in the very New Mills department where he had first been employed in 1940.

He bought his own business – based at the old Martins Bank at the bottom end of Market Street – in 1970, expanding next door sometime later into what had once been the Jubilee Café.

Bill's son, John, now owns the business, so the much-esteemed Barton name is safe for at least the next generation of New Mills shoppers.

Tommy Bowden, Bob Rowlands, Cliff Wild and Harry Ward outside the Church Road Coal Office.

The Co-operative's Black Diamonds float before the parade, 1927.

The Co-op's trusty 'Dennis' dressed and ready for the Thornsett carnival in 1927.

Marjorie Mason opens the Co-operative Drapery on Market Street in 1938. (Courtesy Bill Barton)

Whatever was or was not achieved, however, it is certainly true to say that in 1930 the art of grumbling reached unprecedented levels. During this time of widespread and almost tangible disappointments, many people seemed to conclude that the best – perhaps the only – remedy for relieving their frustrations was a good old-fashioned, get-it-off-your-chest diatribe. Obviously, from time immemorial, public services, high prices, low wages, social privileges and so on had been clear-cut targets for the cannons of disapproval, but now practically nothing was safely out of range.

Motorists berated pedestrians and cyclists for their unpredictability and indiscipline, while cyclists and pedestrians rounded on motorists and their noisy, dangerous, foul-smelling vehicles. Ramblers demonstrated and railed against farmers and landowners regarding exclusion from moorland and dale, while landowners and farmers cursed careless and disrespectful ramblers (such conflicts would lead to the famous Mass Trespass on Kinder in 1932, and the subsequent lionisation of its incorrigible leader, Benny Rothman). Residents complained about everything they could think of – dilapidated roads, dirty streets, malodorous air, inadequate services – and even formed an association of ratepayers to help legitimise their grievances and protect their rights. Electricity – though it had been keenly anticipated – generated a glut of protests regarding the dangers and unsightliness of overhead cables. Football, the darling of the masses, was attacked as 'more a matter of money than of sport' these days. And even the eternal dispute between the poor and the better off was given a new twist. The distribution of poor relief is a good example. For, while many of the more prosperous townsfolk had – on the one hand – both supported the principles and helped establish the practices of providing financial relief for the poor, they could not – on the other hand – bear to see the actual consequences of their altruism: the poor buying vegetables; the poor daring to board buses; the poor chatting and smiling and 'walking through the streets of the town with their heads held high like millionaires'. Why not teach these Torr Top types a lesson, asked one councillor, by withdrawing their benefit for one week? (Proposed but not carried.)

Nor did the weather do much to help. During most of 1930 conditions were, to say the least, capricious – a question of shirtsleeves and flimsy frocks one moment, top coats and heavy wellingtons the next. During spring, skies were grey and thundery and – after what seemed like weeks of snarling and posturing – as summer reached its high point, they finally erupted. Torrential, unforgiving rain lashed down from dense black clouds, to deluge the town and the hills. Man, it was said, was powerless in the face of such a remorseless onslaught. Rivers were choked, the parapets of bridges washed away, huge iron girders unseated from the very fabric of buildings, trees uprooted. 'The swirling waters,' particularly at the bottom of New Mills, 'were terrifying in their absolute fury'.

Salem cottages, Watford Bridge Printworks, Garrison and Beard Mills were inundated, flood waters reached the second storeys of some cottages in Brookside, and a wall of brown slush flowed across the fields and onto Lower Cliff Farm. Many people were driven from their homes, and two men lost their lives as the downpour intensified. Thomas Gannon was

Miss Ashton (later Mrs Beard) with her class at St George's School in 1930. (Courtesy New Mills Library)

drowned near the Windsor Castle lodging house, and John Ollerenshaw died when a sudden swell swept him off his feet and carried him down the valley from the Little Mill Inn, Rowarth, to Bate Mill.

A relief fund was set up immediately, but no amount of money could undo the terrible suffering caused by the storms of the summer of 1930.

It was in this uncertain and sometimes ill-natured and cynical environment that Cyril Bowden would have grown from infancy to adolescence – receiving his education from dedicated but often disgruntled teachers, and no doubt listening, perhaps with growing irritation, to his parents' endless recollections of the old days. At quite an early age Cyril began to develop an interest in bell-ringing and soon became a valued member of the highly respected parish church campanologists. Also, having done very well at school, he was offered an early opportunity to enter the engraving trade, a situation which was, according to his father, just too good to miss.

–oOo–

1938: A doting Cyril dancing to the tune of high romance with Edith, his *inamorata*.

While Cyril, early to rise, will make his daily visit to Campbell's the engravers, Edith will of course clean and polish and cook and shop. Modern advances, however, ensure that she can reasonably expect a domestic life less gruelling than that of many of her predecessors. She may, for example – rather than spend hour after hour tied to the kitchen stove – take advantage of recipes for 'meals in a minute' proffered by her local newspaper and, when it comes to the weekly

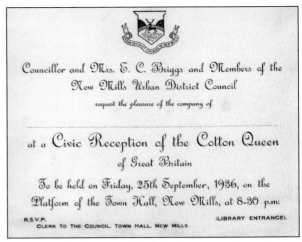

An open invitation to meet Marjorie Mason, the Cotton Queen of Great Britain. (Courtesy New Mills Library)

Marjorie Mason, Queen of Cotton. More than queen for a day. (Courtesy NMLHS)

wash, she may choose the 'easy and economical way', bundling it up, having it collected from her very doorstep, and whisked away to the District Laundry, just round the corner in Low Leighton.

Members of the Bate Mill Bowling Club in splendid form for their group photograph in the late 1930s... carrying on as normal! (Courtesy NMLHS)

'A van will call and we will do the rest.' Very tempting.

There is a golden rule for Edith and her fellow housewives, however, and that is, since the burden of domesticity has been considerably eased of late, they shall never again complain about any aspect of it. For should they so dare, one Marjorie Cooke will all but fry them alive. Observe, for instance, Miss Cooke's contemptuous retort 'To a Bored Housewife':

> Poor Mrs X, I am really sorry for you, because you are suffering from a modern disease, so modern that very few people know the cause... freedom! Frankly (in view of all the new labour-saving devices...) you have too much time on your hands. Remember, every

woman at heart is a Housewife, and her greatest satisfaction comes by being a good one. Ever felt the thrill of other housewives asking for your recipe? No? You poor dear. This is where you start, with a baking day, guaranteed the finest cure for house-keeping boredom in the world.

So, ladies, remember. Be grateful for your lot, smile brightly and labour contentedly.

A second great war seems inevitable in 1938 but then, as the storm clouds lift, it seems unlikely. Then again, impossible. Then probable. And finally, unavoidable. All around you and despite you, a game of likelihood is being played. One thing is certain, however, and that is that you have no say one way or another. You are impotent.

A spectacular photograph by E.R. Morten of a steam train crossing the Torrs gorge in 1933. (© E.R. Morten. Courtesy NMLHS)

Should war break out you will need to be ready to abandon everything. You may survive, you may not. But, for the time being at least, it has nothing to do with you. So just carry on.

Carry on normally. Disregard the portents of crisis.

Pop down to the Art Theatre and sample the Operatic Society's new production – *The Marriage Market*; or go and enjoy the music festival at High Lee, to celebrate the park's first anniversary. Try to get a ticket for the Accordion Serenaders – a group of very talented local lads – at the New Mills Cinema; or visit the Co-operative Society's Trade Exhibition at the Town Hall, where you may be lucky enough to meet the stunning cotton

queen Marjorie Mason in person, and will almost certainly be persuaded – perhaps even by Marjorie herself – that if only everyone would adopt the Co-operative way of life 'the word crisis could be dropped from the dictionary'.

At home, carry on as normal. Read about double-decker buses which might topple over, be warned to 'export or expire', avoid diphtheria and bad sewage, and – should you venture out late at night – please try to dodge the armed man who has been seen prowling around; and do not, whatever happens, get involved in the kind of pub brawling reported during Wakes Week, when – all because of a one-hour drinking extension – 20 separate fights broke out on the pavement in front of the Queens Arms, 'while pandemonium reigned' within!

Think positively. Seek serenity. And try to turn things to your own and your family's advantage. Eat 'Strong and Steady Bread' to calm you, and – should you be fortunate enough to have a garden – create within its walls 'a haven of peace', not to mention a small vegetable patch. And yes, consider vegetables! 'If you are feeling peaky and run down, if you fly off the handle at the slightest thing, why not become a vegetarian?' After all, 'a well chosen vegetarian diet can cure nagging husbands, wives and (even) mothers-in-law of their disturbing tendency'.

Remember also that things could be a lot worse. Think, for example, of the current distress of the Burkinshaws, whose senior member, William – Co-operative manager, organist and conductor of no fewer than 30 performances of the *Messiah* – has so tragically passed away. Consider their grief, and for yourself be thankful.

So... briefly... carry on as normal, eat well, grow vegetables, protect your tranquillity, think positively, stay calm and be thankful... And just one more thing. Let me remind you – should it have escaped your attention – that Mr Chamberlain has been to Germany, has visited Herr Hitler and has averted the threat of war.

The old market ground (now the bus station) in 1935. (Courtesy NMLHS)

By the way... by Sir Martin Doughty

THE OCTOGENARIAN HECKLER – In 1994 83-year-old Benny Rothman, hero of the 1932 Kinder trespass in support of access for walkers to the hills and mountains of the High Peak, returned to New Mills to unveil a plaque on the former police station in Hall Street, where he and fellow trespassers had been held overnight after being arrested.

As Benny started to speak at the ceremony, 84-year-old John Anderson, who had travelled to New Mills from Lytham St Annes, protested that he had been wrongly convicted and jailed, along with Benny and five other trespassers, for riotous assembly.

This bizarre spectacle of one octogenarian heckling another was only ended when the then Chief Constable of Derbyshire, John Newing, stepped forward. Anderson was calmed down by Newing telling him that he believed his plea of innocence.

John Anderson returned to Lancashire with the yoke of 62 years of guilt seemingly lifted from his shoulders.

Benny Rothman confirmed that Anderson had not been one of his fellow conspirators and had probably got innocently caught up in the clash with gamekeepers that had led to the arrests.

MILD MANNERED? - Of the 19 public houses within the parish boundary of New Mills, no less than 12 are tied to Robinson's, the Stockport brewers.

Martin Doughty with Benny Rothman and his fellow trespassers in 1994. (Courtesy Sir Martin Doughty)

While this could be said by some to diminish choice, it has kept alive a tradition which has disappeared from much of the rest of the country – drinking mild beer. In fact, Robinson's mild remains so popular in New Mills that it continues to outsell bitter, the beer-drinker's favourite elsewhere.

THE NEW MILLS GILL

In old imperial units, a gill is a quarter of a pint. But, in New Mills, it was traditionally half a pint. Older pub-goers can still be heard asking for 'a gill o'bitter'.

This local measure was actually incorporated into the New Mills education system. Mr Crawford, headmaster in the 1920s of the Secondary School on Spring Bank (now the Adult Education Centre) used to get his students to chant:

Four gills make one pint
Two New Mills gills make one pint.

One wonders if anything could possibly have been more likely to unsettle you than this onslaught of paternalistic nonsense, particularly since it would seem that in your own day-to-day experiences, the exhortations do not exactly appear to agree with actions being taken.

To illustrate: your council has distributed 8,500 gas masks and you have been warned that they are not toys and must be treated with care; anti-gas instruction is being provided at every opportunity; 20 air-raid posts have been established around the town; arrangements have been set up to evacuate factories; and ambulances and medical resources are being mustered with some urgency. Car owners are being advised that if required they must place their vehicles at the disposal of the council; your beloved hills are being earmarked as emplacements for anti-aircraft gunners, and air-raid precautionary forces are being feverishly recruited. Even the caves and caverns in which you played as a child are being identified as storage chambers for munitions.

And truly, some of those entreaties appear more sinister than others: 'War is ruthless', you are warned. 'Kid gloves are not worn these days, nor are there any ideas of chivalry, such as saving women and children'. Remember how on the playing fields you played to win, 'so now you must face life's real crises with nerves of steel and a spirit of determination'.

So when, towards the end of the year, you are cheerfully assured that the crisis has passed, and when the *Reporter* welcomes 1939 in optimistic mode, you are wise to be suspicious.

Chapter 9
Theatre of War

War memorial

World War Two

bandit has once too often tried to hold us to ransom. [Soon] there will be restrictions [and] hardship, but we need not pull long faces. Life goes on, and it is up to all of us to be cheerful and make the best of things'.

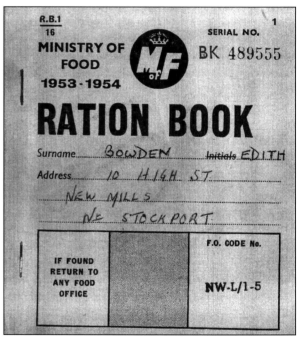

THE sense of calmness, which for so long had eluded New Mills, crept over her with the outbreak of war. It was as though she were a long-suffering patient who had at last accepted – albeit with a mixture of misgiving and relief – that only major surgery could provide a remedy for her malaise.

As war drew near she, the patient, was once again encouraged to 'be of good cheer... the

Perhaps, after all, those relentless months of exhortation and precaution had achieved their objectives, for when the war actually began, New Mills slipped quietly into its ways without panic, hysteria, and without even the slightest hint of jingoism. People seemed determined to make a stand for democracy and freedom. They knew what to do, and what was expected of them.

Circumstances in 1939, however, were quite different from those that had prevailed at the commencement of World War One 25 years earlier. Then, a tidal swell of patriotic fervour had rushed hundreds of innocents to the front, preparations for war had been passionate rather than practical, and the war itself – at least until there were casualties to count – had seemed a distant, disconnected phenomenon; certainly not one to be encountered within the Torrs, or on Church Road or in Low Leighton. Then, there had been no threat of attack from the air – no need, therefore, to mask lights – no fear of poison gas. There had been no wireless to inform and torment people. No first aid stations, or decontamination and rest centres. No air-raid shelters, emergency fire and ambulance services or rescue posts. Then, the cavalry had still formed an important arm of the military, and the government had therefore commandeered not cars and lorries, but horses.

Yet now, in 1939, war was close at hand. It could come from the air, sweeping towards you in the form of enemy bombers or fighter planes, unleashing, perhaps, an assault on the gasholders at Mousely Bottom, or spraying your street with machine-gun fire.

Although it may have been impossible to defend yourself against an enemy such as this, the measures that could have been taken had been taken, and people were as well prepared to face an emergency as they could have been. There had even been dress rehearsals in which they had actually pulled on gas masks, had struggled with blackout exercises, had been encouraged to gather together reserves of food 'equivalent to one week's consumption,' and had even been subject to the unnerving wail of the air-raid siren.

And, almost from the war's opening salvo, Red Cross posts were fully manned, air-raid wardens in position, buildings sandbagged, factory whistles silenced, food and fuel councils operational. Children from far-away places were efficiently housed with their new foster families, air-raid shelters were made ready, and ration books were printed.

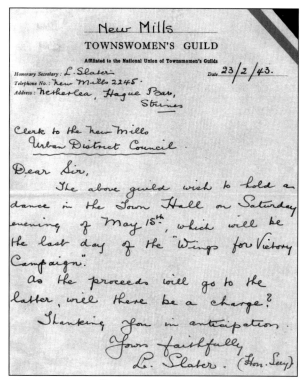

(Courtesy Town Hall)

It was all so very different from 1914. 'Yet, one thing has not changed,' reflected the *Reporter*, 'people are still wondering after 25 years why, with full and plenty for every man, woman and child, men should ever war, or become the victims of overweening ambition, why they cannot live and let live.'

–oOo–

In many ways it was an unspectacular war – though by no means a passive one – for New Mills. People were more at peace with one another than they had been for many a day, and a strong sense of community, engendered by the sharing of a common burden, enabled the townsfolk to fulfil their many and diverse war tasks with distinction. Not once, in respect of her targets, did New Mills fall short. On the contrary, she almost invariably exceeded expectations by huge margins.

Volunteers, ranging from the home guard and the ARP, to nursery assistants, junior women's air corps trainees and ambulance boy cadets, toiled ceaselessly to cover every need and eventuality, to meet every little deficiency that full-time officialdom could not satisfy.

The council's War Relief Fund endeavoured to send parcels for Christmas to each fighting man and woman, and to each confirmed prisoner of war. War

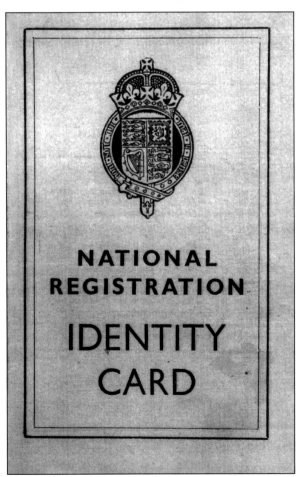

Savings Weeks were supported with astonishing enthusiasm and generosity, producing in total more money than the area was thought to possess!

Having fixed a target of £40,000 for Warship Week, for example, New Mills proceeded to raise £58,000, and was able to 'adopt' a trawler minesweeper, HMS *Spaniard*, for its pains. A War Weapons Week target of £25,000 was quadrupled. Wings for Victory Week, hoping to raise £40,000 – the cost of a Lancaster bomber – actually achieved a grand total of £74,000, almost enough for two! People dug for victory, scrimped and saved for victory, sang for victory, pooled clothes for victory. Was there anything they would not do for victory?

During the war, entertainment became nothing less than one of life's essentials. Yet while evacuees' choirs and ENSA variety shows – the first local version of which was staged at Torr Vale Mill in 1940 – while these managed to tempt many people from their firesides, it was undoubtedly home entertainment – and particularly the radio – which truly captured the population's hearts and imaginations, and acquired what today we would call cult status. Sandy Macpherson, Vera Lynn, Tommy Handley – not to mention Ali Oop, Mrs Mopp and Colonel Chinstrapp – lifted the nation's spirits so much that not even Lord Haw-Haw, try as he might, could dash them.

Whenever the opportunity arose, newspapers, too, adopted a bright and breezy manner, and often included children in their deliberations. Rationing might serve as a case in point: with the approach of Christmas 1942, Uncle Ben – whose famous Children's Corner was never one to be daunted by adversity – invited his young nieces and nephews to write an essay describing what

High Lee Hall. (Photo: Stephen Lewis)

were the very best things about Christmas rationing. There would be a five shillings prize for the winner.

Wrote one small niece:

> In one way not having rich food is a blessing in disguise. No getting up in the middle of the night for mother to dose sick children with castor oil.

Wrote one tiny nephew:

> If being rationed and going without toys means that we shall have a quicker victory... then, hurrah! for a rationed Christmas.

Yet far from being funny and trivial, the war was in point of fact a nasty and deadly affair. Losses among the fighting men and women of New Mills, though lower than in World War One, were nonetheless heavy, and seemed heavier still since they could not be borne in isolation. Added to the casualties of World War One their weight must have been unbearable. And, since for an entire generation, conflict – conflict past, present and future – cast an inescapable shadow over people's lives, it must have begun to seem that war was a natural condition, and that the years in between had been nothing more than an intermission between two acts of the same epic tragedy.

As for aerial bombardment, though the High Peak was not a prime target, her proximity to Manchester and Merseyside created for her an ever-present threat. A small number of raids – indiscriminate rather than cleanly targeted, distressing rather than materially harmful – had taken place during the first phase of hostilities, but it was not until 3 July 1942 – when two German aircraft swooped over New Mills and Hayfield, raking villages and farmland with bombs and machine-gun fire – that civilian lives were lost and buildings demolished. Although attempts to strike the Mousely Bottom gasworks and the railway viaduct failed, two houses together with the Methodist Chapel in Low Leighton were destroyed. Ten-year-old Joan Handford, who was playing the piano in one of the houses, died immediately, while Daniel McKellar, the chapel caretaker, was so seriously injured in the blast that he died in hospital the following day. Before being shot down the planes streaked on to Hayfield where six villagers – including four members of one family – were killed when Spring Vale Road was bombed.

–oOo–

On 8 May 1945, Mr Churchill announced, 'The German war is at an end. Let us have a brief period of rejoicing – then Japan.' Accordingly, rejoicing for the Victory in Europe commenced. New Mills was 'lavishly and prettily' decorated with flags and bunting that had lain uncared for in basements and attics for too many years.

The question of celebrations, however, had exercised people's minds for a long, long time. For how could one truly rejoice in the shadow of such horrors as the war had exposed, and when what should have been a new dawn in Europe was neutralised by the continuing darkness in the east?

Some weeks before the day of victory the *Reporter* had commented:

> The return of heroes of ancient history... was celebrated by strewing their path with roses. That has gone forever [for] the gods have taught the war makers that war is not a sport, but enemy number one of the human race. When the news of the cessation comes, surely the uppermost feelings will be of thankfulness and relief. We can hardly express that relief with flag waving and bonfires.

A few bonfires were lit however, and a few flags waved. There were parties and church services, and bells were rung. The council sent a message to the King, and a telegram to the Prime Minister. At High Lee Park, the children of New Mills were each presented with a commemorative sixpence, and al fresco teas – cakes and sandwiches, custard and ice cream – were served to the accompaniment of Jimmie Fox's band. Meanwhile, down at the Market Ground – though this was an isolated case of delirium – 'Hitler's coffin' was burned amid cheers and loud guffaws.

Little more than a month later an announcement concerning the Bowden family appears in the local newspaper. It welcomes home Eric Bowden of the Royal Engineers, and mentions a brother, Corporal F. Bowden, who continues to serve with the RAF in Egypt.

Cyril Bowden, however, a bombardier in the

The coach house, High Lee Hall.

Royal Artillery, shared neither his brothers' nor indeed his father's gift for survival. Cyril had been killed in Holland a few months before in January 1945, leaving his wife, Edith, and a young son.

Postscript for Cyril and Edith Bowden

The whole of Cyril's life was dictated by war – aftermath, preamble, deed and consequence – and following his death, in 1945, Edith would never speak of his experiences. After the war she took a ladies and babywear shop at 10, High Street and lived to see the new

Schooldays. Cyril, bottom left. (All items courtesy Elaine Bowden)

millennium. Cyril and Edith's son, Allen, died at the age of 55 in 1996.

WALTER CAMPBELL & Co., (Engravers) Ltd.   Established 1881.   Telephone : Works, New Mills 2115
Telephone : Residence, New Mills 3221.

(Directors : J. W. Cochrane, J. Cochrane.)

Mrs. C. Bowden,
Meal Street,
New Mills.

ENGRAVING WORKS,
NEW MILLS,
Nr. STOCKPORT.

5th February, 1945.

Dear Mrs. Bowden,

May I on behalf of the Soldiers' Comforts Fund Committee extend to you our very sincere regrets on hearing of the death of your dear husband.

Cyril was a very dear friend of ours and was greatly esteemed by all who knew him as a loyal and courageous man.

At these times there seems to be little comfort to be had, but we feel sure that with God's help you will find strength and courage to carry on. You have a fine little son who needs your help and love and we pray that God will bless you both.

Yours sincerely,

Jean C. Cochrane — Hon. Secretary.
Soldiers' Comforts Fund Committee.

The letter of condolence from Cyril's employer.

Edith with her son, Allen, and her mother.

Edith and Cyril. A summer stroll in Paignton.

Chapter 10
In the Pink

WE PUSH on towards the middle of the century. Once more in search of a land fit for heroes. Or even for unremarkable people like ourselves. Almost everything is in short supply.

We are short of food: bread, biscuits, tea, and meat. At Christmas time there are so few provisions to be had, that Mr Foy – though the shortages are hardly his fault – is moved to issue a statement:

> I am sorry that the first peacetime Christmas cannot be celebrated with unlimited quantities of Christmas fare, but regular customers can be assured that poultry, rabbits and fruit will be shared out on an equitable basis. With

the dawn of a peaceful New Year I look forward to an early return of good things for the table, and I take this opportunity of thanking customers for their patronage and patience throughout all the difficult days.

We are short of clothes. Our coupons are low. Fashion bazaars, to display and sell new designs, are out of the question, so we introduce bring-and-buy sales. At first we make them into big occasions and include opening ceremonies with speeches, but we soon dispense with formality since we are more than impatient to pounce on the jackets and dresses we covet from the corner of our eye.

We are short of fuel, and in the winter, muffled against the blustery snow, we trudge down Market Street, towing a child's sledge behind us, and queue for our coke allowance outside the gas showroom. To make matters worse, in 1947 there is a seven-week storm throughout February and March.

We are denied, and feel deprived of, those things that people in the cities and large towns have – hospitals, maternity homes, and swimming pools. Yet we cannot have them since our town is too small. It is, we are told, an 'intermediate town,' and we must be prepared to share facilities with Marple or Whaley Bridge.

We seem to need so much. In order to assist the

Mr Ratcliffe and Mr Bowden with employees of Watford Bridge Printworks. (Courtesy David Williamson)

timekeeping of the buses which wait on Union Road, for example, it is evident that we need a public clock. True, we do have a perfectly splendid clock on the Town Hall tower, but that is beyond Hall Street – 'miles away' from the waiting buses. Once again we are told that we cannot possibly have such an amenity, and that we must make do with the tiny clock in the window

Mr Bowden and Mr Ratcliffe... 'wedded to an industrial tradition'. (Courtesy David Williamson)

than later. Additionally, although it is indeed true that our electricity supply is the envy of our neighbours, we should not allow that to divert attention from our failures.

We are short of a job, of industrial and commercial investment, short of training programmes. Yet by an odd twist of fate we are also experiencing a shortage of workers with specific expertise in a number of areas, and we cannot fill existing vacancies. We have, for example, very few weavers.

While we are also inevitably short of young men, our schools are short of children. In 1901 there were over 1,200 pupils in our elementary schools. Now, in 1946, there are a little over half that number.

Yet we do have 628 residents who are over 70 years of age, and who are about to receive, or have received, gifts of foodstuffs from various parts of the British Empire. One recipient, it is reported, gazed at his food parcel in utter amazement. 'I didn't know I knew anybody in Australia,' he said.

–oOo–

Perhaps we are just too impatient. Wanting everything at once. If only we could be grateful that the war is past. If only we would forbear, and accept that things both locally and nationally are better now.

It is not as dark as it once was. Can you remember, indeed how could you forget, the barren and menacing darkness a few years back? But look now.

Come into the street and you can see that at night New Mills has been turned into a fairyland. Look at the lamps overhead. Night has almost become day. Look even to the distance, to the

of the Union Road post office, which will soon be synchronised with wireless time.

And since we are talking about buses, it has to be said that we are in dire need of a bus station with adequate shelters. At the moment there are no shelters at all on Union Road, and people have to creep into doorways when it rains.

We are short of car parking facilities. During certain periods of the day one can hardly move for motor cars; and there have been several altercations between irate shopkeepers and the drivers of vehicles who have parked erratically.

We are short of good, safe and reliable gas and water supplies, and, incidentally, the Gow Hole water question should be addressed sooner rather streams of light, necklaces of light, reaching out over the hills. What would you have given for such a vision only two or three years ago?

Can you imagine, two, three, five years ago, bemoaning the absence of a public clock? You would have been thought quite mad. Can you imagine taking up arms on behalf of a car park, or because of the lack of bus shelters, or because it is beginning to seem likely that you will have to share swimming facilities with a neighbouring community?

And can you image denouncing New Mills as unsightly and declaring her – as some have just recently done – 'an ugly picture in a beautiful frame'? Of course not. Your dissatisfactions in the late forties are evidence enough that things are a good deal better than they were!

Meanwhile, from the darkened stage of the Art Theatre, one can detect whispered endearments and occasional outbreaks of actorly irritation. For, after several years of enforced inactivity, your local operatic society – that much loved micro-cosm of artistic and political intrigue – is once again beginning to stir. In order, however, to re-establish its impressive tradition of light operatic performances – a tradition which, you may recall, had begun in 1922 with *The Gondoliers*, and had ended somewhat abruptly in 1939 with *The Maid of the Mountains* – a fund of at least £100 will be required.

Raising such a large amount will not be easy, and so, in addition to jumble sales and raffles, the dramatic arm of the society will stage a number of modest, fund-raising 'tasters' – *The Blue Goose*, *The Quiet Weekend* – in an effort to tempt you back into the theatre you would once have visited so naturally.

Finally, resources and props having been assiduously gathered, auditions squabbled over, and rehearsals consummated, a fully costumed version of *No, No Nanette* will be presented under the skilful stage direction of Norman Nestor.

Nanette herself will be yours for the taking on 5 December 1952 – providing you are prepared to pay an admission price of anything from half a crown to six – yes six – shillings. A little expensive perhaps? But there it is! If you wish to behold an outstanding spectacle of a dozen delightful dancers, or to tap your feet to the 'capable orchestra' conducted by Percy Ratcliffe, to witness a production in which 'no one falters, misses a line, or drops a cue,' and if you will be dazzled by a shock of ultraviolet light coruscating on billowy white dresses, then, up to six shillings is the price you will have to pay. No argument about it.

–oOo–

There is, not far from the parish church, an attractive cottage for sale. It boasts parquet floors, entrance hall, morning room, larder, small cloakroom, lounge, kitchen, three bedrooms and a bathroom. It is 'excellently appointed'. It is a 'refined, artistic, tasteful and luxurious property,' one which 'should be examined to be fully appreciated.' While – at £2,000 – it is expensive, it could be considered a very wise investment.

How odd it is to turn so abruptly from utility and depletion to luxury and investment; to playing with property and making money. Perhaps this is the way ahead – a glimpse of a new psychology, or at least one which has been until recently stifled by a society compelled to make-do-and-mend. And – certainly in the case of property transactions – there is even a fresh use of language to help lead us forward; one with a

The making of Bakehurst. (Courtesy John Hemsworth)

touch of ambivalence about it – a delicate balance of euphemism and hyperbole. 'In need of slight improvement', 'a compact second bedroom', 'delightful views to the side', 'a rare opportunity to purchase'. It is obviously a kind of market language, and, in future it may be that – particularly if this sort of thing catches on – we shall have to learn to read between the lines.

The cottage by the church – and others like it – was also significant in another respect, for it represented exactly the kind of property – high quality constructionally, middle of the range economically, unpretentious socially – which would enable New Mills to move away from her largely industrial past to a more residential future. Here, in the fifties, such a move seemed both logical and prudent. For although New Mills was undoubtedly 'still wedded... to [her] industrial traditions,' circumstances did appear to be 'compelling her to develop in other directions'.

Consequently once again (for this had previously happened in the mid-19th century) her residential qualifications were wheeled out, dusted down, discussed and advertised at every available opportunity. Given her profusion of cultural and sporting facilities, her trio of railways, her surfeit of bus routes, her provisions for education, her beautiful surroundings and her innovative, not to say imaginative council – given these things you might easily conclude that New Mills was the very model of residential desirability.

Such conclusions, however, were by no means consensual. For in some areas of the town housing was still trapped in an underworld of dereliction, and the people who lived there were angry and frustrated. To them the very thought of a residential haven with luxurious cottages was deeply offensive. It was a tense situation, one which required positive action – perhaps a champion. Someone tireless and dedicated to the thankless task of fighting to improve the conditions of the poorest members of the community.

History obliged in the person of Dr Leslie Millward.

Dr Millward was – like Hibbert, Mackie and Godward of days gone by – one of the real heroes of New Mills. His almost evangelical style had been demonstrated on his election to the council in 1946 when he had referred to his new colleagues as 'the twelve,' and had devoutly hoped that there would be neither 'a doubting Thomas, nor a Judas' secreted within the assembled company. For there was work to do.

A general practitioner, Dr Millward had held the centrally situated Redgate practice since before World War Two and – since many of his patients came from the Torr settlements – he had gained ample experience both of the terrible diseases – diphtheria and tuberculosis – that period-

ically oppressed the area, and of the dreadful living conditions that exacerbated them. Even by 1949 only one-third of the houses in New Mills had baths, and less than half had flush toilets. New housing, therefore, became his imperative.

Housing development was to be a long and expensive venture, and at almost every stage it seemed that delay followed delay. Tractors and diggers broke down, politicians wrangled, money ran short, severe weather intervened, developers procrastinated. On one occasion – on the Highfield Estate – although it was hard to admit, progress had not gathered pace until German prisoners of war had set to work.

Dr Millward constantly tackled the most awkward of issues with passion and resolution, and, although he did not work alone, he was both the spark who ignited a hundred projects, and the flame which kept them alive. He gained benefits and allowances for the disadvantaged, pushed ahead with slum clearance schemes, pressurised planners and managers, harangued and sometimes exhausted his associates, and, no doubt with an occasional modest glow of satisfaction, watched the houses rise.

In 1949 to help temporarily relieve the housing shortage, 50 'prefabs' were erected at Highfield, while between 1948 and 1955, nearly 400 permanent houses were built – many at Highfield, and others at Diglands and High Hill. And how delighted the parish church must have been to find the town, at last, virtually on its doorstep!

But – inevitably one supposes, since some people are very strange aren't they? – not everyone was happy! In fact rather than jump for joy at the very sight of these clean, bright, spacious, draught free, healthy, toileted, bathroomed, be-gardened dwellings, a number of people could only object

More houses are added at Bakehurst. (Courtesy John Hemsworth)

because some of the buildings were finished off in beige or pink! One ex-serviceman was heard to comment, 'I didn't fight this bloody war to live in a pink house... New Mills is grey and always will be'. Well, yes, pink isn't really New Mills is it? Yet one cannot help but believe that many of those who complained did so largely because, over the dismal years, they had simply forgotten how *not* to do so!

At the same time, Dr Millward's medical practice grew and grew until, in 1952, he accepted a partner, Dr Andrew. Dr Millward's energy was, apparently, boundless, and his work with the council (sometimes as chairman), with the Housing Committee, with his patients, the cricket club and his church, with the Civic Amenities Society – he was instrumental in the restoration of the Torrs – all such things still allowed him the time to become captain of the Golf Club!

Dr Millward died in 1982, and two years later the oaken footbridge spanning the River Sett was opened by way of celebrating his life's work.

New Mills in Winter by Gary Wood

The River Sett and the Millward Memorial Bridge.

Torr Vale Mill.

The Torrs Millennium Walkway, opened 1 April 2000, winner of the Derbyshire Greenwatch Award.

The Torr Mill weir and Church Road Bridge.

Bridges of the Torrs spanning the River Goyt.

The Hall Street Library

New Mills Library – the Carnegie Free Library – stands on Hall Street, almost opposite the Old Constabulary. An annexe to the Town Hall, it is an unpretentious building quite free of Edwardian pomp and circumstance. True, it is a stone edifice, and yes, it does boast a touch of the Classical, but any sense of severity is averted by its 'informal' hilly position, surrounding trees and disarming architectural detail.

Christine Howe, librarian 1974–1995. (Courtesy Christine Howe)

The evolution of the present institution is, to say the least, circuitous, with roots reaching back to the New Mills Peoples' Institute of 1852, and the Market Street Mechanics' Institute (1860). Suffice it to say that the library's immediate predecessor – located in what is now the Council Chamber of the Town Hall – was opened by the Duke of Devonshire on 30 September 1899.

As regards users' conduct, rules and regulations – at least as they appeared in the first library catalogue of 1905 – they were rigorous. Browsing, for example, was not permitted. Instead, borrowers were required to prepare and submit a list of 20 books 'in the order wanted… as many of them may be out at the time.' A messenger would be sent to collect books not

The building of the Hall Street Library, 1910. (Courtesy John Hemsworth)

punctually returned (at the borrower's expense), and borrowing while suffering from infectious diseases would incur a penalty of up to £5. Concerning the Reading Room, persons in a state of intoxication, persons 'uncleanly,' or persons suffering 'offensive diseases' were barred; neither sleeping nor audible conversation were permitted; and, finally, should violations occur, a constable would call and offenders could expect to serve up to six months in jail.

Kath Dent, Barbara Matthews and Gwenda Culkin 'in situ'.

Despite such draconian legislation demand grew and grew, and it soon became clear that a larger building would be required. The new library would be built on land donated by Henry Barber, the then chairman of the Library Committee, while Andrew Carnegie, the Scottish/American industrialist, would contribute £2,000 to the project. The Carnegie Library was opened on 25 June 1910.

Happily, over the generations, practices and regulations have been modified, and nowadays,

The library. (Photo © Gary C. Wood, 2003)

for both adults and children, the library is a relaxing, hospitable and stimulating place. No concept here of 'thought in cold storage'; no feeling of the dry, the dull, the dusty. This is a place of discovery, of exhibitions and 'Bookchat'; a place where even the technology is friendly; a place with a staff of such enthusiasm and knowledge as would cause even Barbara Pym's 'excellent women' to lose heart!

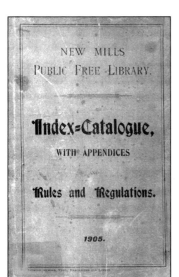

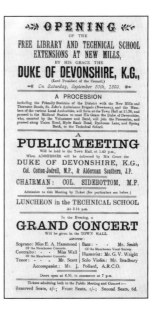

Rules and regulations! (Courtesy New Mills Library)

Chapter 11
New Elizabethans

AS WE have watched history marching or dancing or shuffling along, we have observed the people of New Mills town in many frames of mind. We have spied upon their communal grief, upon their communal rejoicing, and now – since this may be the very moment to do so – we shall present ourselves at what could be the occasion of their communal convalescence. For it would seem that at last there is a sense of cheerful expectation in the air.

Recalling days gone by one is struck by how important a role public occasions have played in the uplifting of our town's communal psyche.

Over the centuries New Mills has achieved many things, but truly her celebrations have been among her brightest glories. Perhaps what was needed now was a festival or a great historical pageant to bring the people together in a high-spirited whirl of self-indulgence.

And behold! The early 50s brings forth two such opportunities: the Festival of Britain in 1951 (which we shall allow to pass), and of course in 1953, the crowning of Princess Elizabeth. Now while the death of King George had been a sad business, one wonders could history have possibly found a more timely moment for a new Elizabethan age?

Suddenly, as if by spontaneous combustion, committees, sub-committees, working parties spring into action. Every group, organisation, sect, club, institution, society, is hungry to be involved. Cubs, Scouts, Guides, Brownies, the Rotary people, Young Mothers, the Masons, works groups, the Townswomen's Guild, the British Legion, the Birch Vale Glee Club, bands and choral societies; churches, schools, youth and sports clubs; the Foresters, the Red Cross, police and firemen. Not to mention the Chrysanthemum Society, Toc H and the Ancient Order of Shepherds! 2 June will be a date to remember.

The council, for their part, will obviously play a pivotal role in both promoting and coordinating what promises to be an elaborate programme of events. How ironic that they have only recently

Something to celebrate? (Courtesy Town Hall)

been roundly criticised for initiating evening dances in the Town Hall! 'It is hardly dignified,' puffed an opponent of the scheme, 'for a public authority to become regular dance promoters on a commercial basis.' Yet now they can employ the expertise thus gained to everyone's advantage.

There are many ideas, proposals, questions. About, for example, the illumination of New Mills; about the route and scope of the town procession; the nature and themes of the historical tableaux. About street decorations – where is the civic bunting? – bonfires, campfires, beacons, fireworks, flaring torches (isn't it strange how celebrations and fire intermingle so readily?); about street parties, square dances, drawing competitions, tug-of-war teams. Will the council be providing souvenirs for the children? Of course. Mugs for the under sevens, propelling pencils for the sevens and over! And what about tea parties

for the general public? Obviously. And, before you ask, yes, 'even people over 65 will be included.'

And now, just as preparations are reaching their zenith, someone, somewhere, hesitates. And thinks, and realises that – wait a minute – this is not 1837 or 1918, this is 1953. This is the age of television, and it may be that not everyone will be that keen to stand waving flags or to leap around the streets in amusing costumes, when they can see the whole show in the comfort of their sitting rooms with a lettuce sandwich and a nice cup of tea.

Debates arise. Organisers canvas their members. People with 'no say' are asked to say. What is the role of the traditional town parade in this age of television? Will you join in the celebrations? Will you march? Can we count on you for the egg and spoon race?

Organisations waver. Council members drum

Summer 1953. A Coronation feast at the Town Hall for the new Elizabethans. (Courtesy NMLHS)

their corporate fingers, and scratch their corporate heads. And finally – broaching no argument to the contrary – the council acts. In an endeavour to ensure that no one misses the spectacle, they install television sets in halls, old folks' homes and other institutions. Electrical shops run out of televisions.

At length the promised day arrives. It is grey, it is misty, it is dreary. It is raining. It is the most miserable of days, and for the entire duration of the royal cavalcade and the crowning ceremony itself, the streets of New Mills are virtually deserted.

In due course a few figures begin to appear, and some of the planned events begin to recover. There is a torchlight procession and a bonfire. There are some fancy dress and sporty happenings. In the evening, New Mills is illuminated, and handsomely so. A Coronation Concert is said to be

'fairly well attended,' and certain organisations are praised for putting on 'brave shows' under the circumstances.

In actual fact, however, 2 June 1953 represents a major triumph for the little box of pictures in the corner, and one cannot help wondering whether the concept of celebration is changed forever; whether our new Elizabethans will become devoted but passive subjects of the new medium, rather than active members of the community, and whether our so-called communal convalescence will now be managed from a television studio in Alexandra Palace.

–oOo–

During this period – according to the official town guide at least – New Mills appears to be a remarkably well-regulated and well-serviced community, rich in industrial enterprise, abundant in educational opportunity, and teeming with clubs and societies.

But how do these glowing images translate into reality? Do they 'stand up' at street level, and do the townsfolk of New Mills live together peacefully, with a measure of satisfaction?

Up to a point, they do! Since, however, anxieties are never too far below the surface, many people continue to experience some apprehension as regards certain aspects of the evolving world. What exactly is a hydrogen bomb? Or the Cold War? And how does an Iron Curtain actually work?

Yet, frankly, the majority of their concerns are of a far less elevated kind, many of them revealing more than a touch of the over-familiar.

The perennial matter of Wakes Week for example! For astonishingly, notwithstanding generations of argument, the pattern of the Wakes holiday has still not been settled. Do we opt for a fortnight in July,

New Mills through and through! (Courtesy Town Hall)

or in September? Or perhaps one week early, one week late? And how can it be that a proper workable solution has still not been found? Indeed, by now would it not be more sensible to address not the niggling details, but the very concept of the Wakes holiday? Whether or not it could be considered, in this day and age, an anachronism to be discarded forever?

A much-disputed proposal to introduce Sunday soccer also has a familiar ring. That people should be free to enjoy fun and games on the Lord's day, is received with stark indignation by some. It would be bad for the image of the town, say the protesters. Bad for football too, and an affront not only to the Lord himself, but to the whole of Christian society. We should conserve what little decency we have retained, respect the day of rest, and keep it holy.

There are also concerns of a less familiar kind; little irritating issues, reminders of the less palatable trifles of the contemporary world. It is, for instance, becoming aggravatingly common to discover lipstick – yes lipstick – smudges on tea cups and drinking glasses. This is, of course, not only unhygienic, but disrespectful to one's fellows. And the matter, according to the parish magazine, does not end with cups and glasses. There have been smears on the chalice.

On a more serious note there is the matter of street crime and disorder: on the one hand, gangs of ruffians making their way round the town after dark, leaving behind them a trail of destruction; on the other, the spectacle of strange figures loitering in shadowy doorways, hair oddly sculpted, trousers tight as a snake skin, long jackets with velvet lapels; causing mayhem in the cinema or the dance hall; their passions inflamed by rock 'n' roll. They are called teddy boys. But it makes no sense. No sense at all. So, yes, there are concerns, but for the time being at least, they are marginalised by a general glow of optimism which appears to lift the spirits of the town.

The shops are fat with foodstuffs and clothes, and with shiny appliances. People have never

The Pineapple Inn dressed for the Coronation in 1953. (Courtesy Town Hall)

dreamed of garments of such high quality – bewitching dresses, sumptuous Nicholson overcoats, flattering ready-to-wear dinner suits; and they have never imagined such delightful furniture – wardrobes with lilac doors, high-gloss dressing tables with veneered walnut tops. They are thrilled by twin-track tape recorders and by 17-inch television sets (with tubes and valves freely replaced when necessary). Sweets have been de-rationed and cafés – such as the very popular Jubilee – are groaning with reckless, teasing cakes, with Titterton's succulent pork pies, and mountains of prize-winning Cheshire cheeses. The local Co-operative Society might well complain of falling sales due to customers' 'growing habit of making a Saturday outing to one of the big shopping centres', but to see Union Road and Market Street on Saturday morning, one would never guess.

Also, though the doubters might not remember this, it is a matter of great satisfaction that after a generation or more of instability, many local businesses – order books bulging – are working beyond capacity, and some are even offering weekend overtime at generous rates. Yes, it may be true that this flourish of prosperity will not last, but for the moment, such is the demand for goods and services that, in their search for employees, three New Mills companies have engaged West Indian workers from Manchester, and others are looking to do likewise.

At the same time, 'Mr Swizzel' (Michael Dee), and Mr Matlow – confectioners supreme – obligingly redefine the term 'long service'. Accordingly, whereas many companies will still require employees to wait 40 or even 50 years for their gold watches, at Matlow's and Swizzel's the prize will be earned after a mere 25. And it need not be a gold watch! Recent long service gifts have included radiograms, sewing machines, and, in one case, a mink cape.

–oOo–

It could perhaps easily seem, however that the fifties lack 'edge'; that both locally and generally very little actually happens, few things change; that it is a time devoid of real colour and energy, and is neither here nor there. Certainly, in retrospect it suffers by comparison with the shamelessly ostentatious sixties, an era which may inadvertently have stolen its thunder. Yet it could be that our vision is blurred, our hindsight imperfect, and that there is more to the fifties than meets the eye. Indeed, further reflection upon its exploits and achievement might well reveal a surprisingly dynamic and complex profile.

It was an age of space exploration: sputniks, space suits and images of the dark side of the moon; an age of ever-advancing earthly technology: delta-winged bombers, the sound barrier, atomic submarines, universal television, popular air travel; of all kinds of domestic improvements: refrigerators, washing machines, spin dryers, frozen foods, canned beers. It was an age for youth, 'modern' culture and leisure: rock 'n' roll, skiffle, long-playing records and disc jockeys; and an age of good old-fashioned human endeavour: the four-minute mile, the ascent of Everest; and inevitably an age of wars, revolutions and power shifts: Korea, Hungary, Suez and the demise of the British Empire.

It was in the fifties, however, that Britain's long and dreary phase of utility and austerity came to an end, and it did not seem entirely unreasonable in 1959 for the Prime Minister to remind us that we had never had it so good.

Princess Diana's celebrated visit to Swizzels Matlow on 14 June 1990. (All items courtesy Swizzels Matlow Ltd)

Sweet Success

It must have been a great day for the children of New Mills when Swizzels came to town. Think of it, a giant sweet factory of your very own! And in the 1940s too, when it may have seemed that only bad things could happen.

The yellow van with blue mudguards. A heart-warming sight for children everywhere.

Swizzels Ltd – formed in 1933 from two existing companies, one run by the Matlow brothers and the other by David Dee – moved to New Mills to escape the London Blitz.

It was a happy move, and in the grey days of post-war Britain few sights could have been more welcome than Swizzels' bright yellow vans with their distinctive blue mudguards. As the

Swizzels, leading the way!

Company expanded, old mills would be reborn, thousands of people – many of whom would give a lifetime of service – would find employment and distinguished industrial awards would be won.

In 1975 the company would become Swizzels Matlow Ltd, and today, a generation later, the Dees and the Matlows – still guiding lights – can look back with some pride on their families' achievements.

Matlow Fruities. Four for one old penny!

The late Mr Maurice Matlow receiving the Queen's Award to Industry from the Lord Lieutenant of Derbyshire, Sir Ian Walker-Okeover, in June 1971.

A view of the new Swizzels Matlow factory, completed in 1971.

Chapter 12
The Swinging Sixties

Albion Mill.

The Union Road cinema. (Courtesy Derek Brumhead)

THE Swinging Sixties! And overnight New Mills is transformed into an oasis of mind-expanding drugs, free-flowing sex, and the music of peace and protest; a haven for the promiscuous, the unworldly and the politically ingenuous.

On certain Saturday afternoons – weather permitting – traffic is disrupted, and shoppers, deeply curious, stand and stare as sweetly-scented processions of mildly spoken mystics – bearded, bangled and garlanded in flowers – float along Market Street towards Foy's Corner.

They are mostly, though not exclusively, young and willowy, barefoot or sandaled. Children, many children, skip along beside or among them,

glowing with innocent happiness. Petals are strewn on the ground from raffia baskets, bouquets of wild flowers are offered to onlookers, guitars are strummed distractedly, and artless songs of love and liberation fill the air. Lean, handsome bearded men – hair down to their shoulders – seem aloof and almost holy, while long-legged, flimsily clad young women clasp rubescent babies to their bare breasts.

Light heartedly they make their way up the steep incline of St Mary's Road – old men with walking sticks, factory workers in boiler suits, elderly ladies with heavy baskets, in their wake –

The New Mills School six-a-side football team of 1968. (Courtesy New Mills Library)

and assemble in High Lee Park, their Elysium, to recite poetry, smoke their delicious pot, and make love randomly in the long grass.

But where are they from, these gentle innocents with their anomalous American accents? Birch Vale? Ollersett? Or even, perhaps somewhere beyond Hayfield? Yet Mr Bagshaw of Laneside is there, as is Miss Spenser from Eaves Knoll – acutely mini-skirted. There too are Mrs Bowen and Mrs Booth, surprised by their own rashness. Rolling their eyes, clapping their hands and making love instead of war.

This, then, is New Mills in her Age of Aquarius – indulgent, permissive, and three sheets to the moorland wind...

I tell a lie! For although it must be that in some ways the heady, sensual sixties impinged upon New Mills' consciousness, there is little or no evidence for it. She has no memory of it. And we can do little other than speculate and make images of her moody and amorous excesses.

–oOo–

Peace and friendship, however – though in a quite different way – did claim New Mills' attention at this time.

Although 20 and more years had passed since the end of World War Two, many of the older townsfolk had been left with a painful, and in some cases bitter, legacy. Generally speaking, however, it was believed not only that it was high time to move on and to leave behind old animosities, but that some active steps should be taken in the name of reconciliation. For how can it be possible to find peace within oneself and one's community, if inwardly war is still raging against one's former enemies? Can we forgive? Ought we to try?

New Mills School and Sixth Form Centre, a winter view. (Photo © Gary C. Wood, 2003)

A glimpse of High Street.

It could not have been easy, yet, regardless of the hostility that some people must have felt, and of the disapproval of others who regretted the financial costs involved, the project not only survived but went on to enjoy conspicuous and lasting acclaim.

The transformation of Salem Cottages.

It was in this context that the twinning of New Mills and the mediaeval German market town of Alsfeld was initiated. Some people were sceptical. They could not help but wonder about the benefits, or if you like, the follies of such a manoeuvre: of inviting young Germans into their homes – in some cases the very homes in which evacuees had taken shelter; of welcoming German boys and girls – and in turn being welcomed by them – with bands and choirs, and the flags of two nations ; of the children of their enemies singing *Auld Lang Syne* on the school lawns of New Mills; and of their own sons and daughters performing *Romeo and Juliet* in the Alsfeld Klostergarten, presumably in the belief that if anything could speak of peace and understanding, then music and drama could. Who could have imagined, only a few years before, finding complimentary references in local newspapers to 'our young ambassadors from Germany', and to the happiness engendered by their visits?

In other spheres of activity that confidence which had characterised the late fifties held fast for a number of years at least. At the beginning of 1965, for example, many local industries were booming, and some firms were in a position to refurbish and expand. The company based at Torr Vale Mill, already employing 200 workers, invested in 24 brand-new Swiss looms, each of which could weave five towels at any one time. Night shifts were introduced to handle the consequent increase in capacity.

Fanfare for Alsfeld

Romeo and Juliet, Alsfeld, 1964. (Photos courtesy Lynne Woodward)

And industrial progress was only one part of the story. Evidence of renewal could be found all over the town; nothing spectacular or revolutionary, just quiet, modest improvement. The badly corroded prefabs on St George's Road and Ollersett Avenue were being phased out and replaced by rows of bright bungalows; a community centre and laundry were being built near Mrs Peel's and Mrs Lockhart's houses in Bakehurst, and many of the ancient and ramshackle cottages of Torr Top were finally being brought down, thereby making way for the long-awaited shoppers' car park. Hall Street library was preparing a section for the lending of long-playing records, a Civic Amenities Society was taking shape, and a new club house for senior residents – Sett Valley House – was under construction.

Football – though not necessarily Sunday football – was exultant! Thanks were due to the Millers' extraordinary manager, Joe Martin. For it was he who masterminded what became known as the golden age in the club's history. So revered was Mr Martin that his name was sometimes mentioned in the same breath as Shankly and Revie. Under his guidance New Mills Football Club was well nigh invincible, for 10 years or so capturing trophy after trophy with alarming regularity.

At the same time members of the Operatic and Dramatic Society – having been left homeless by the cinematic demise of the Art Theatre in 1959 – were campaigning hard to raise money in order to lease the theatre on a temporary basis; while the council were actually discussing the possibility of initiating a Civic Theatre to help reverse what they perceived as a decline in community spirit.

One could, perhaps, see the council's point, for on the darker edges of New Mills, teenage hooliganism entered one of its more intemperate phases. Taking to the streets and transforming them into some kind of adventure playground, a small but potent number of young people began to personify a gap between generations which – primed with intolerance on both sides – could summon no compromise. Whether justly or not, the words teenager and hooligan became synonymous, and the elders could find neither the language nor the tone to broach an ever-widening chasm. The young would no longer be lectured, the old would not be defied; and it must have been very hard for those in authority – whose word had for so long enjoyed total domination – to find their orders and reprimands drained of substance.

Yet what can be done when rebellious teenagers set fire to narrowboats moored along the canal, or smash the windows of the Thornsett Band Institute? When they break into Hobson's Café, or harass old people in High Lee Park? What do you do? Do you wag a reproachful finger? Denounce the Welfare State? Do you deplore the indifference of parents, the laxity of the police, and the leniency of magistrates? What action can you take when they ransack your post office, vandalise traffic bollards, and kick out the bus station windows? Do you despair, or concede that hooliganism is as old as the hills? Do you rattle your sword, or reach out to the offender, enter his theatre of strife, and appeal to his better nature? It is a predicament.

In an ordered community it is a predicament when dissident groups hamper people's lives and curtail their pleasures. In the middle sixties, for example, it became virtually impossible to enjoy an evening at the cinema, since the hooligans had determined to make it their own. They would pour ammonia on the floor, slash the seats and the screen, empty the fire extinguishers and break the toilets. They would chase each other up the aisles and into the foyer, tumble out onto the pavement and roll into the road.

It is a particular predicament for Mr Corbett, the cinema's hapless manager, who, as the unruly behaviour escalates, is totally perplexed. He cajoles, pacifies, threatens and fulminates, but nothing seems to work.

Finally, in desperation, he announces closure and, predictably all hell breaks loose. The cinema? To shut down? How dare he try to intimidate us, rant the hooligans. Where can we go? How shall we spend our evenings?

On the eve of the final curtain, enraged beyond measure, the teenagers take matters into their own hands and stage their last and finest bloody battle – a strategy so fruitful that the cinema, bowed and battered, is quite unable to re-open in order to close, as planned, on the subsequent night.

A GREAT RIOT ON THE EVE OF CLOSURE... VICTORY FOR THE LOUTS, roars the *Reporter*.

Mr Corbett, subdued but resolute, gathers together his belongings, saddles up swiftly, and drives out west to concentrate on his other – far less alarming – enterprise, the Regent Cinema in Marple where, it is said, behaviour is much, much better!

And so it passes that, just as in the fifties a few wayward teddy boys had put an end to the Town Hall's popular dances, the lawless rockers of the sixties – in an act of self-defeating folly – propel the cinema, with its dreams and memories, from here to eternity.

But the rockers have not yet played their trump card! They do so in an almost surreal postscript, in which, in order to persuade Mr Corbett to reopen their beloved arena, they organise – incredible though it might seem – a protest riot in which they sweep through the streets of New

Mills in glorious revolt! In the mêlée, 40 teenagers, including five young girls, are rounded up, and 19 of them appear at the courthouse to face an array of charges.

Even in the best of societies such things are likely to happen, and although the rockers' revolt was by no means trivial, neither was it representative, for while the rebels were claiming the headlines, the vast majority of teenagers were creating stories far less newsworthy. Most of them in fact were both puzzled and offended by mindless behaviour which cast aspersions upon them too. For in the evenings the majority of young people would watch television, visit friends, or perhaps call in at the New Mills Youth Centre for a game of football, cricket or netball. They might play darts, draughts or dominoes, organise a visit or tea party for the elderly or for disadvantaged children, practise judo or weight training. They might set up a fish and chip supper social, and dance to their favourite pop records.

In fact it is worth recalling that at the very height of the swinging decade, New Mills Youth Centre could boast a membership list of over 400 youngsters.

As you might imagine, however, no amount of statistical evidence could quickly repair the damage caused to New Mills' reputation by her hooligan minority, and as the sixties petered out, although efforts were made to repair relationships, and to reaffirm the many positive aspects of the town, it must be said that the shadow of the few hung over her streets for some time to come.

For a number of other reasons too, New Mills approaches the last third of the 20th century in fairly low spirits. Programmes which have been set in motion to improve her rather glum and neglected appearance – the planting of rose bushes near the Mason's Arms, and trees in Redmoor Lane – have hardly begun to take effect. Similarly, Dr Millward's ambitious riverside project – conceived under the auspices of the Civic Amenities Society – to transform the lifeless banks and dangerously polluted waters of the Torrs into a thriving place of beauty and recreation, has made, as yet, little progress. The irresistible decline in her manufacturing base cannot be disguised by sporadic industrial revivals, nor has that decline been counterbalanced, at this time, by viable alternatives: residential enhancement, the development of service industries or tourism. The profile of the community itself lacks coherence and a sense of equilibrium in its population, its aspirations and outlook. Youth is at a crossroads and, as young people leave by the score, their departure accentuates an unpropitious tilt towards the elderly. In-comers, on the other hand, have neither quite grasped the spirit of their adopted domicile, nor have they acquired a sense of empathy as regards her history. Traditional benefactors – steeped in civic responsibilities and good deeds – are dying away, and the new settlers – often middle-class professional people – may require a community quite different in ethos from that of the past.

Redundancy, unemployment and lack of opportunity – exacerbated by half a dozen industrial collapses in three years – create insecurity, suspicion and rancour among the longer-established population. Taxes, rents and fares are on the rise, the railways – notwith-standing proposals for a new station to replace Central – are economically vulnerable, and the Hayfield Line is bound to close. The grammar school is to become comprehensive – an advantage, no doubt, in the longer term, but one which cannot immediately be recognised.

The sixties, bright, liberal and idealistic in their pubescence, inconsistent and unsteady in their middle years, tend, in their dotage, to dash the hopes and expectations which had been assigned to them.

Carnival

1977–8 would be the happiest year of Karen's life. She would attend dances and galas, parties and gymkhanas and – conspicuous among her memories – a torchlight procession through the village of Tideswell. She would present prizes, draw raffles and open bazaars, and would be,

A carnival float. (Photo courtesy New Mills Library)

above all, an important ambassador for the town that had made her queen.

When New Mills carnival committee was formed in 1974 it had a specific job to do: a mission to raise funds for a town swimming pool. It was a popular cause and when in June the first carnival parade crawled through the crowded streets, it seemed even that the weather – stiflingly hot – was keen to help. Just six years later, the new pool – standing back from Hyde Bank Road – was opened to the public, and though many agencies contributed to the project, much credit must go to the carnival, its personalities and the unflagging workers.

Karen (now Karen Morris), had been crowned in the summer of 1977, a year of true carnival fever. On Saturday 18 June, hot air balloon ascents and a

Karen Morris, the retiring carnival queen with her attendants, June 1978.

mediaeval pageant thrilled the crowds who had gathered, after the procession, on the field at Watburn Road. There was a fun-fair with side-shows, a fancy dress parade, the judging of decorated floats and shop windows, and – who could possibly forget?- a 'welly chuckin' competition'. And in the evening Alex Welsh and his band had set up a Dixieland feast in the marquee.

But for many people the most memorable event would have been the crowning of the queen.

The New Mills carnival programme 1977. (Courtesy Karen Morris)

At 1.05pm precisely, Karen was taken by boat from Bowaters to the Newtown Marina, where, at 1.40pm, she would have joined the Carnival procession. Two hours later she would have received her crown from retiring Queen Lynn, who would speak emotionally of 'memories to last a lifetime'. And so, as the company rocked and jived the night away, Karen began a year which would seem to pass in moments, and in no time at all it would be summer, 1978. She would be watching the 'world famous' Don Lindbergh dive in flames from a high tower into six feet of water, and Penny, her successor, would be beginning a whirlwind reign.

Gradually the New Mills carnival lost its momentum and it was discontinued in 1982. Reintroduced in 1997, it seemed to have recovered its sense of purpose but sadly, by the close of 2002 its future was in doubt.

Town, Torrs and bridges. An aerial view of New Mills. (Courtesy Bill Barton)

Chapter 13
Theatre of Living Memory

DEAR Reader, the generation from 1970 to the year 2000 and a little beyond, is probably familiar territory to you: a theatre of living memory, so to speak, with private experiences, comedies and tragedies, friends and families.

If during the course of that generation you have lived in or have otherwise known New Mills, she will no doubt have played a role – be it prominent or insignificant – in shaping those experiences. She may even represent the principal context for them – a context so personal that you may feel further interference from an independent commentator such as myself to be quite inappropriate.

Nonetheless, since I can hardly abandon my story at such a moment, herewith some scattered recollections – to complement your own – from this eventful, ever-accelerating age.

–oOo–

Gusty winds driving through the hostile, rubbish-strewn Torrs, whipping up clouds of polluted foam from the surface of the poisoned river, and tossing them into the air. Dr Millward and his colleagues gradually redeeming the deadly gorge's worst features. The growing awareness of heritage and environment, and the painstaking evolution of the Torrs project.

The dissolution of the New Mills Urban District Council in 1974, the setting up of the Town Council in its place, and the incorporation of New Mills into the Borough of High Peak.

Proposed extensions of the scandalous land-fill site at Mousely Bottom, strongly and successfully opposed by the youthful Martin Doughty together with his tireless band of allies. Grappling with the

Market Street. (Courtesy The Buxton Advertiser*)*

horrors of an abandoned gas works, a scrap-yard, a sewage farm, a toxic landscape. Convoluted land purchases, the planting of 22,000 trees; and Councillor Doughty becoming, in many people's eyes, a worthy successor to the good doctor.

An elaborate pageant staged in the summer of 1984, complete with an elegant Victorian street parade – to mark the centenary of the opening of the Union Road bridge; and, immediately afterwards, the proud inauguration of the Millward footbridge down in the Torrs near the meeting of the rivers.

The superb restoration, in the 1980s, of the Art Theatre, which had been purchased 20 years earlier after an exhausting fund-raising campaign by the Amateurs.

The establishment of the Heritage and Information Centre in 1988, above the Torrs in a converted butcher's cellar; a centre representing material acknowledgement of the town's commitment to regeneration and environment, and providing a focal point both for visitors and for the New Mills Local History Society whose activities, prolific and scholarly, have added so much to the area's self-knowledge and self-esteem.

'New Mills 600', a glorious commemoration – held in 1991 – of the very first recorded reference to 'Newmylne' six centuries earlier; and the planting of oak saplings at Mousely Bottom, by 600 schoolchildren.

And inevitably, over the years, memories of countless events, people, places and experiences of far less consequence. Some of no consequence at all.

Dreary evenings, perhaps at the ephemeral Bingo Club on Union Road; and occasional visits, long ago, to the mobile cinema; Mr Foy bequeathing his greengrocery business to Mr Peel,

The Co-operative's drapery department on Union Road in 1970. (Courtesy New Mills Library)

an employee of 42 years; watching the paint dry on gaudy narrowboats in the Newtown marina; catching a glimpse of the famous steam roller; practising scales and arpeggios in the little music studio on Albion Road; enjoying, retrospectively, bonfires and firework displays which at the time had seemed tedious; skimming through the *Town Crier*; ridiculing the very notion of tea dances; wondering where the old police station had gone, and discovering a new one on Hurst Lea Road; wallowing muddily in the One World Festival; visiting Billy Bigelow and Orpheus down Jodrell Street – Billy on his fluffy white cloud, Orpheus in his frisky underworld; stalking Baskerville's hound in the woods near St Mary's, and chasing Gismo's golden ball along the river bank.

As for the town's controversies, one, of course, took them to heart – though, perhaps, in a 'third person' kind of way: the community hospital debate; the Market Street facelift; the question of parking bays and traffic-calming schemes; the interminable saga of the by-pass; the relocation of the council's market. And the architectural commotion regarding the new law courts adjacent to the Town Hall. Was the proposal for their design inventive and daring? Or was it breathtaking in its insensitivity, compounding, so to speak, 'an error of taste with one of judgement'?

However diverse our reminiscences of the last

Hunting the beast of Ollersett Moor. (Courtesy The Buxton Advertiser)

New Mills School: retirement of headmaster Albert Read in 1979. (Courtesy New Mills Library)

Ann Wyatt, weaver, Torr Vale Mill, 1993. (Courtesy NMLHS)

30 years may be, one aspect of the period – its major theme perhaps – must surely have affected us all: the growth of technology.

–oOo–

By the year 2000 the revolution is a fait accompli, and many of us – usually those of 'a certain age' – have all but fallen by the wayside. For, after a tentative few years, technology has surged forward in wave after wave, in a frenzy of information and triple-w-co-dot ingenuity, from which there is no escape.

Many of us have felt uncomfortable, many under threat, particularly in the area of professional credibility. For although in the past we have confidently held our own, we are now floundering

in a mysterious universe. Quizzically, we are stared at by sharp-eyed, quick-witted colleagues who can be no more than 23 or 24 years old, and who communicate – at least with each other – in a language quite different from our own.

And when company strategy is discussed we find ourselves gazing at a proposal from Metatron of Union Road – www dot metatronuk dot com – which robs us of our capacity to respond… a proposal that future success will depend upon launching our company into cyberspace! Further, a counter-proposal from Digital Insight – an organisation far too progressive to proffer a terrestrial address – identifies a redesigned web as our first priority. The choice makes matters worse for us! What shall we do? Opt for the mysteries of cyberspace, or for website redemption? Frankly, we have no idea.

New Mills School: the 1979 hockey team. (Courtesy New Mills Library)

Albert Sedgwick, Queens Garage, Union Road, 1993. (Courtesy NMLHS)

The Kinder Handbell Ringers

The Kinder Handbell Ringers of New Mills, an all ladies team, joined the Handbell Ringers of Great Britain in 1981.

In 1988, after a busy programme of fund raising events, the team acquired a fine new set of Whitechapel bells. The photograph (above) shows leader Anne Hopley and Margaret Sidebottom at the Whitechapel bell foundry.

The handbell team in 1985, performing at a rally in New Mills.

The winning MacWives in 1982. (Photos courtesy Christine Howe)

Punkwives of 1986.

XYW

The New Mills Young Wives Group was formed in October 1970, and long before the new millennium they had become – in their own words – 'Ex-young wives' (or as they neatly appear in print, XYW).

Today – together with their new members – they are as alive and high-kicking as ever, enjoying a varied diet of social, cultural and of course charitable events. Whatever the occasion – stage shows, carnivals, barbecues, reflexology sessions – the merry wives will be there.

The Eagles of 1971. Phil Dent is on the bike, Graham is second from right. (Photos courtesy Graham Dent)

Wayne Pendleton, Graham Dent and Alan Sealey, in dead earnest.

Young Eagles

In 1980 New Mills Cycle Speedway Club, the Eagles, staged no less an event than the British National Finals.

The choice of New Mills for such an important occasion represented a conspicuous accolade for Graham and Philip Dent who, together with a few like-minded enthusiasts, had formed the club 10 years earlier, and had been involved in every aspect of its fortunes.

In 1970, in response to the boys' requests, the council had provided a piece of land at Picker Brook, upon which an oval shale-covered track had been built in readiness for the 1971 season. Before long the Eagles were riding to Manchester league victories, but two years after its opening the track was destroyed by flood water and evacuation was the order of the day.

In due course, however, again with council assistance, a new track – a track fit to stage the British Finals – was built on part of the Newtown recreation ground.

Yet, despite their dedication and their successes, despite even an optimistic merger with Offerton Cycle Speedway Club in 1982, a new generation of riders failed to emerge and, in 1984, the young Eagles were finally grounded.

A little embittered by our newfound illiteracy and our apparent inadequacy, we begin to remark upon other ways in which our dear old town is changing according to the demands of modernity. In High Street, for example, we can obtain Gatineau skin care, Phytomer body treatment and a St Tropez false tan. In High Street! Can you imagine Vernon Hughes or even Mary Higginbottom with a false tan? Alternatively, down Church Road, close to where Bill Hodgson had his grocer's shop, we can now purchase 'the total look', complete with racoon extensions.

And yet, in the way that one's eyes become accustomed to the dark, we gradually begin to make out familiar shapes in the shadows. And even as our juvenile colleagues surf the triple w oracle for the meaning of life, or boldly stride out to polish and glamorise their bodies at the Leisure

The Hudsons, father and son, Ollersett Hall Farm, 1993. (Courtesy NMLHS)

*Torr Vale Mill (Higham Tongs Ltd). The mill yard in 1993.
(Courtesy NMLHS)*

Centre solarium, or tighten their biceps at her state-of-the-art fitness centre – even as they reach, via cyberspace, for the stars – we begin to discover, at ground level, a few timely reassurances: Messrs Barton, Dowell, Foy and Wilks, who between them can claim over 200 years of service to the village shopper; Potts, our local baker, whose proud boast is to have been established in New Mills for over a hundred years; Chafes, the solicitors, who have witnessed the events of Market Street and Union Road since 1889; and Lorrell's who have provided a quality photographic service to local people for 35 years. Even Swizzels Matlow – New Mills' largest employer, and a true www dot company if ever there was one – aspires to be regarded as a 'long established family concern'. And, oh, how we are consoled by the familiar-sounding names of their products – Love Hearts, Fizzers, Rainbow Drops and the rest – and by the evocative candy smells that invade our nostrils, just as they did when, in our childhood, we crossed the Albion Road bridge.

Again, even when we invite our friends to a pub lunch or an evening drink, how many of us will choose the Waltzing Weasel's 'traditional' bar – free as it is from music, machines and mobile phones? Or the Pack Horse with its 'traditional' beer garden and real ale; or the White Hart, the Royal Oak or perhaps the Swan with its 'traditional' Sunday roasts and blazing open fires? And how is it that in our self-consciously post-post-modern world traditional things are so widely valued and urgently advertised?

–oOo–

For our final glimpse of New Mills we shall return to the Torrs – the town's most potent expression of continuity and intent.

Jim Thompson's High Street shop.

Entrance to Torr Vale Mill. (Photo: Barbara Matthews)

While the Torrs – or 'the park under the town' as it is known – represents an impressive monument to the past, it is by no means a mausoleum. For it is also a place of recreation for today, and, in many ways, an inspiration for the future.

As for the past, down in the gorge we can re-appraise the dreamers and engineers of old; industrial patriarchs and their workers. Benefactors, pretenders, politicians. Authors of the future. We can commend waterways, embankments and bridges; or pick over the ruins of those Georgian mills that generated history.

Or we can shift to the present. Chase kingfisher and wagtail; scale steep rock faces that rise up to Torr Top; tickle trout in the dashing waters of the river once known as the 'liquid leper'. Or perhaps just walk… for mile upon mile… the sandstone gorge, Goytside meadows, the River Sett trail, Mousely Bottom, the parade of bridges…

Jim Thompson in 2003, his 25th year on the High Street.

will they retrench? When artists make sketches and national newspapers take pictures, when torch light processions gather round and brass bands sound fanfares, will they smile or frown? Will they approve when the Royal Mail strikes a millennium walkway stamp, when radio and television companies make programmes of celebration, when helicopters packed with distinguished architectural judges pay respectful visits and she wins auspicious prizes? Will they be impressed when, during millennium year, 200,000 people descend into the gorge to admire her?

And how will they like it – those spirits of the past – when the 'park under the town' begins to revive that confidence with which they themselves

marvelling at the inscape of a land retrieved from exhaustion.

And the future? What symbol might we choose to best represent New Mills' future? My own choice would be clear: the Torrs Millennium Walkway.

Catch her on a bright spring day glinting in the sunlight. Curving tautly round the battle-torn gorge. The 'missing link'. An incisive, upbeat upstart, displaying to those grandiose elders round about, an easy 'stroke of luck' charm they can but envy. And embodying, at the same time, the very best of those well-rehearsed New Mills affections – ambition, imagination, tenacity.

But how will the walkway's venerable neighbours – the bridges, mills and embankments, the spirits of New Mills past – how will they respond to this charismatic newcomer? Will they open their minds as if to a new opportunity, or

Alan Wilks. The family have had shops on Market Street for 50 years.

The weavers' shed fire at Torr Vale Mill, 2001. (Photo: Peter Beardswood)

Indian dancers at the annual New Mills One World Festival, 2001. (Photo: Peter Beardswood)

had once fired the engines of New Mills' ambitions?

But, more important still, how do you regard the New Mills of today? For it is, after all, your perceptions that will seal the town's fate. You will decide how well or badly New Mills has performed; will approve or disapprove of her actions. You will have been encouraged by her triumphs and angered by her failures. You will judge when she has been less than positive or too hasty; when she has served you well and when she has let you down. It is for you to say whether New Mills has languished in the remnants of her industrial past, unable to advance – her wisdom a tired and outmoded one – or if she has successfully adapted, with imagination and resolution – to our rapidly advancing world.

'Crown Imperial'

'Crown Imperial', an exhibition of commemorative pottery and china dating from 1817 to the present day, was held at St George's Church in May 2002, as part of the Queen's Golden Jubilee Celebrations. 'A chronicle of our national heritage', Crown Imperial represented

'Coronations, Jubilees, Royal Weddings and other great historical events'. Beautiful – and often most delicate – items of porcelain, many featuring royal portraits, were displayed in the handsome setting of St George's, together with pictures, objets d'art and exquisite floral arrangements.

(Photos courtesy Barbara Matthews)

The Nesbit Connection

Jenny Agutter's visit to the 'Three Chimneys' cottage on Cobden Edge

Gwenda Culkin, Jenny Agutter and Barbara Matthews outside 'Three Chimneys' on Cobden Edge. (Courtesy Barbara Matthews)

Edith Nesbit, 1858–1924. (Courtesy The Nesbit Society)

must have brought much satisfaction to Gwenda Culkin and Barbara Matthews, for it would have helped underline the significance of their discoveries regarding author Edith Nesbit, her novel *The Railway Children*, and the New Mills area.

And, just as Ms Agutter will always be identified with her role as Roberta in the 1970 film version of *The Railway Children*, perhaps Barbara and Gwenda will be remembered for solving the long-standing mysteries of the story's locations.

New Mills Dance and Theatre Centre

The New Mills Dance and Theatre Centre has been operating for 15 years and Carolyn Dent, the centre's charismatic director, can now boast 350 students. Here are the senior and junior modern teams of 2003.

(Photos courtesy Carolyn Dent)

The Summer Festival

Fire is no stranger to New Mills. Both town and Torrs have known its cruelty. But fire, like water, is a dual element. A force for ill or for good.

Imagine then, a summer's night, the Torrs alive with music – the rhythms of samba – and with fire. Not the flames of destruction, but of celebration. There is a procession of perhaps a thousand people, many with lanterns: serpents, fishes, stars and planets. A dragon? A phoenix? Children and their grown-ups 'ooh' and 'aah'. The Millennium Walkway glimmers from the flares below it and the lights upon it.

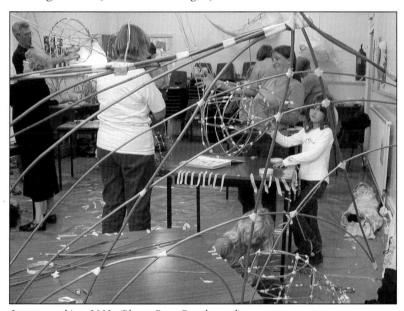

Lantern making, 2002. (Photo: Peter Beardswood)

The flames of celebration. (Photos: Peter Beardswood)

Above, the walls of the Torrs and the face of the mill flicker unsteadily. Down the river's calmer waters there are lantern towers and waterlilies of fire, while the Torr Mill weir is incandescent, lit from within. Eventually the procession reaches the park near Torr Vale Cottages and, after a few moments… the fireworks begin!

But this is not some strange pagan ritual. It is the climax of the 2002 New Mills Summer Festival, a lively and spectacular event which has included in its varied programme lantern-making workshops led by Karima Ellis, one of the creators of those amazing willow and tissue lanterns which so enthralled Commonwealth Games audiences.

The Summer Festival was launched in the early 1990s, the brainchild of Mike James, then head of New Mills Secondary School, and has since become an annual feature of the local calendar. It is an imaginative, inclusive and relaxed event, a mixture of cultures and media,

with activities as much at home on the street or in the pub as in school, church or Town Hall. And, although it offers a host of celebrities, it is as much about taking part as being entertained.

And yes, it *is* imaginative. A train ride to Edale accompanied by a Jewish folk group? Poetry with pasta? Still life classes? A battle of 'rock' bands? A spot of ringing and singing? An exploding custard? Romanian Dancing? Or a cup of tea with 'greenfingers' at the Grange? The summer festival has it all.

It is, as the organisers had always hoped it would be, a high-spirited affirmation of the adage, 'fun for all'.

'Force Five' at St James's Church during the 2002 festival. (Photo: Philip Kendall)

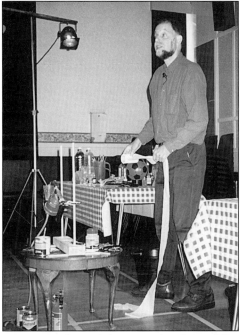

Dr Ian Russell, 'Exploding Custard'. (Photo: Philip Kendall)

History and Heritage

Few places can have been better served by their local historians than New Mills. Formed in 1982, the Local History Society celebrated its 21st anniversary in May 2003, its very survival a tribute both to the energy and enterprise of its members, and to the quality and relevance of their scholarship.

Functioning at first under the umbrella of the Civic Amenities Society, the local historians soon

Jane Butterworth and Mo Cohen at the centre.

chose to seek independence, and became, a year after their foundation, a free-standing organisation. Financially unsound, however, to make ends meet members decided to publish small booklets of their research activities. And so was established what became a definitive collection of history notes and other publications which have so painstakingly recorded and helped interpret the life and times of New Mills and its surrounding areas.

Ron Weston, Derek Brumhead, Roger Bryant and John Humphreys, four local historians whose publications and enthusiasm have helped bring the history of New Mills to life. (Photo: Barbara Matthews)

But there is much more to their Local History Society than its publications. Each year they devise and implement an impressive programme of talks and exhibitions, walks and excursions. Indeed, it would seem that the Society is prepared to leave no stone unturned, no will or deed unread, in the interests of the better understanding of New Mills' tantalising history.

–oOo–

Formerly a butcher's basement, the New Mills Heritage and Information Centre perches above the Torrs near Rock Mill Lane. Independent from, yet closely linked to the Local History Society, the centre has been administered from its outset by the well-known local historian and writer, Derek Brumhead. Officially opened by broadcaster Brian Redhead in Spring 1989, the centre is a treasure trove of local photographs, documents and artefacts.

A child-friendly mine tunnel, a slide show and an elaborate model of New Mills in 1884 (complete with an expertly composed commentary) are among the special features

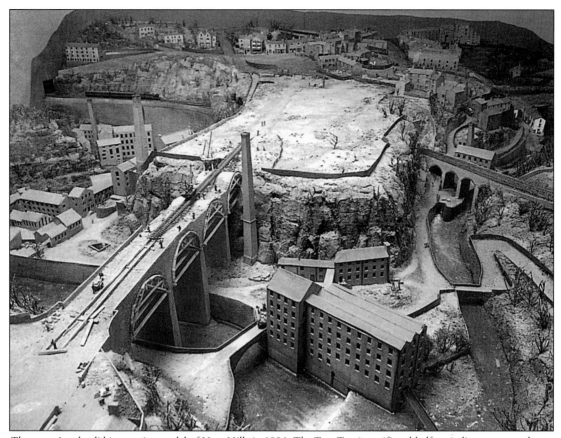

The centre's splendid interactive model of New Mills in 1884. The Torr Top 'massif' and half-encircling gorge can be clearly identified. (Photo: Derek Jones)

which complement an ever-changing archive of exhibits. Children come to sketch and study, walkers drop in to peruse the books and leaflets, and behind the counter a capable team of helpers provide an engaging prescription of informed advice and hot coffee. Ideal!

Marion Williams, Brian Redhead and Martin Doughty at the opening of the New Mills Heritage and Information Centre on 8 April 1989. (Courtesy New Mills Library)

References

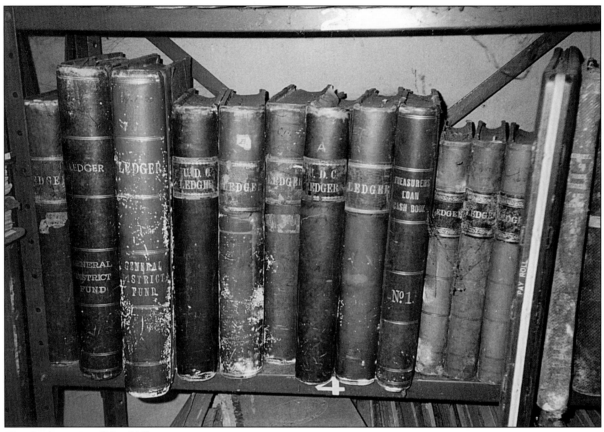

Here lie the stories of New Mills...

D. Brumhead, *Railways of New Mills and District: Their Development and Impact 1840 – 1902*, Lancashire and Cheshire Antiquarian Society, Vol. 86, Transactions of the Society, 1990.

D. Brumhead and R. Bryant, *A Short History of New Mills*, New Mills Heritage Centre, 1993.

D. Brumhead and R. Bryant, *The Torrs Riverside Park Bridges Trail*, New Mills Town Council and Derbyshire CC, 1987.

R. Bryant, *Turnpike Roads and Riots, (New Mills History Notes No. 7)*, New Mills Local History Society, First Ed. 1984.

R. Bryant and J. Symonds, *New Mills and District – A Look Back*, New Mills Local History Society, 1987.

D. Brumhead, R. Bryant, R. Weston (ed.), *New Mills. A Look Back at its Industrial Heritage*, New Mills Local History Society, 1997.

O. Bowyer, *The Torrs and Peak Forest Canal – An Historical Trail*, New Mills Heritage Centre, 2000.

G. Culkin and B. Matthews, *The Nesbit Connection – Edith Nesbit Literary Trail*, Derbyshire Leisure and Heritage Dept, 2000.

M. Doughty, *The Millers*, 1974.

M. Doughty, *The Town Under The Park – The Making of the Torrs Riverside Park*, Derbyshire CC Libraries and Heritage Dept. 2001.

H. Froggatt, *Caddie to Captain to Veteran*, New Mills Golf Club, 1996.

P. Gee (ed.), *Thornsett, 1878 – 1978*.

J. Humphreys, *New Mills Co-operative Society, 1860 – 1890 (New Mills History Notes No. 20)*, New Mills Local History Society, 1989.

S. Lewis, *A Debt of Honour – Men of the Sett Valley*, S.P. Lewis.

J.A. Pearson, *Duties of an Urban District Council Surveyor*, New Mills UDC, Heritage Centre, 1996.

J. Powell, *The Hayfield Union Workhouse (New Mills History Notes No. 27)*, New Mills Local History Society, 1999.

J.H. Smith and J.V. Symonds (ed.), *New Mills, a Short History*, Manchester University Extra Mural Dept, 1977.

J.V. Symonds, *The Mills of New Mills*, New Mills Local History Society, 1991.

J.V. Symonds, *The Torrs Industrial Heritage Trail*, Derbyshire CC.

M. Tebbutt, *Centres and Peripheries: Reflections on Place Identity and Sense of Belonging in a North Derbyshire Cotton Town, 1880 – 1990*, Manchester Region History Review, Vol XIII, 1999.

S. Warburton, *History of New Mills Golf Club*, New Mills Golf Club, 1979.

R. Weston, *New Mills 1835 – 1839 (New Mills History Notes No. 18)*, New Mills Local History Society, 1988.

R. Weston, *The New Mills Tithe Award (New Mills History Notes No. 9)*, New Mills Local History Society, First ed. 1985, Second ed. 1988.

A Brief History of the Art Theatre, New Mills.

New Mills 1894 – 1994, New Mills Town Council, 1994.

The High Peak Reporter – various editions.

The Buxton Advertiser – various editions.

New Mills Official Town Guides – various editions.

The New Mills website – www.newmillsweb.com (Peter Beardswood).

Old Ordnance Survey maps:

New Mills (Newtown) 1896 , Derbyshire Sheet 8.02.

New Mills (Low Leighton and Beard) 1896 , Derbyshire Sheet 8.03.

Birch Vale 1896, Derbyshire Sheet 5.15, The Godfrey Edition.

Index